# Heart and Hard Work

JAMES D. MILLER

# *Heart and Hard Work*
## Memories of "Nordeast" Minneapolis

GENNY ZAK KIELEY

NODIN PRESS

ISBN: 0-931714-77-X


Nodin Press, a division of Micawber's Inc.
530 North Third Street
Suite 120
Minneapolis, MN 55401

JAMES D. MILLER

This book is dedicated to my mother,
Mary Agnes Zak, who believed I could write
even before my pen ever touched the paper.
*And*
To my husband Doug and my sons Joe and Andy
for the things they have taught me about life.

*We would like to acknowledge the following publications for giving permission to use the articles that appear in this book:*

Brian Anderson "Mayslack's: Roast Beef and Ethnic Trimmings" (Minneapolis Star and Tribune April 8, 1973).

Don Boxmeyer "Al's Place" (St. Paul Pioneer Press March 3, 1991).

Amy Clements "Grain Belt Brewery Tour Illuminates Northeast Building's Colorful History" (Northeaster Sept. 24, 1986).

Tim Fuehrer "Early Edison: Vaudeville, Popcorn, Sunlight Dances, Sodas at Schrags" (Northeaster May 17, 1989).

"Heart Centers of Minneapolis" (Minneapolis Tribune March 9, 1924).

Frank O'Brien "Skating Pleasures of Early Days" *Minnesota Pioneer Sketches* (Housekeeper Press, 1904).

Imogene Erie Schopf "63-Year-Old Lowry School Closed: Reminiscences of a School that Won't Open this Fall" (Minneapolis Argus Aug. 16, 1978).

Glenda Shaffer "Voice of Memory Recalled of Logan Park" *Over the Years at Logan Park* Minneapolis Park and Recreation Board (Omega Press, 1992).

Brenda Ueland "What Goes On Here" (Minneapolis Times Jan. 21, 1944).

Joseph Zalusky "The East-Side Fire: The Tragic Day, August 13, 1893, When Part of Minneapolis was Devastated by Fire" (Hennepin County History Spring 1960).

# Appreciation

JAMES D. MILLER

In the past two years I learned that the real history of Northeast is not to be found in textbooks, but can only be discovered in the heads and hearts of its people, information that has been passed down for generations. It is my hope to preserve these memories. The fourteen personal recollections of Northeast residents were chosen randomly. But I did try to give a cross section of different ethnic groups.

I am grateful to those who answered countless questions, shared memories, photographs and in so many cases gave me the gift of their genuine support. At the conclusion of this book I came away happy to know that tradition and a sense of pride in Northeast still continues.

My heartfelt appreciation goes to Marion Kozlak, J. Sam Misencik, Stew Thornley and Alan Ominsky for their encouragement and genuine "go for it attitude" when I first started this project.

I would like to thank my friends at The Writing Center for their continued attention and support. A special thanks to Meg Miller who worked as a consultant and is to be commended for her dedication and excellent work.

In the last year I lost two of my dearest friends, Nancy Doerfler and Maureen LaJoy. They not only encouraged me on a regular basis to write this book, but actually helped me to write it. Nancy is credited with writing almost the entire chapter three on churches of Northeast. And Maureen, my teacher helped me to see my vision clearly. These two women are in heaven now and deserve to be. It is not easy to share someone else's dream. They were planters of seeds and I will never forget them.

# Contents

*My mother and I in the backyard about 1957.*

*Gramma and Grandpa with uncle Eddy in front of our house on California Street, taken in about 1924.*

# 1 A Northeast Childhood

## My Family

My mother Mary Agnes was born on Fifteenth and Marshall Street in Northeast Minneapolis, the first of her family to be born on American soil. Her parents John and Agnes Koniar came from southern Poland, the region of the Gorali people, who were known for their music and colorful folk art.

My grandparents worked hard and eventually saved enough to build a small, sturdy house. Built in 1915, the Koniar house was the first one on the block of California Street in old "Nordeast." Later, as the family got larger, more sections were added on to the original house. My grandparents also took in boarders to make ends meet.

As a little girl, my mother told me stories about my grandparents. So, although they died before I was born, I felt their constant presence in my life. She told me about how my grandfather would often take a walk to the Gluek's Brewery beer garden on Twentieth and Marshall Streets for a free glass of beer. She talked about her memories of quiet times when Grandpa would take his children to Columbia Park to pick strawberries, flowers, and mushrooms. She bragged about how my grandmother's bread served with pavidwa, a prune butter, was the best on California Street.

## My Own Upbringing

My introduction to Northeast Minneapolis took place at the tender age of six. After the death of my father, my mother decided to move from our small farm just north of Little Falls to the Twin Cities. After her personal loss, returning to the neighborhood where she had been raised must have comforted my mother. But this new place offered no consolation to me. Compared to the country, the city houses stood too close together, and the harsh sounds of the city traffic frightened me.

Through my young eyes my grandparent's barn-shaped house seemed unwelcoming. The yellowed stucco appeared dull and old-fashioned. Inside the house, the furnace reminded me of an octopus with metal arms stretching to the ceiling, while a trap door opened to a dark basement coal room, and a dangerous stairway with no railing led up to the attic. The attic contained things I considered junk: army and navy uniforms from World War II, old wool coats and quilts, inexpensive holy pictures on the walls and two old trunks that my grandparents brought from Poland in 1904.

I figured I could never learn to love the community the way my mother did. But my mother assured me that I would learn to love my new home and, as usual, she was right. However, my opinion toward my new environment shifted only gradually. As the days passed, I began to feel more at home as the people and places of Northeast became familiar to me.

The first years of my life in Northeast, I stayed within a small radius of home. Everything I needed was within an easy walking distance. I spent a great deal of time at Schiller School and Marshall Terrace Park. My family went to St. Hedwig's Church, which

*Church of St. Hedwig's 29th and Grand NE 1925.*

was just four blocks away. The drugstore and dry cleaners were located close by on Lowry Avenue. And an A & W Root Beer Stand, a shoemaker, and Ptaks Clothing Store were just two blocks farther from those businesses. Favorite weekend spots included the Ritz Theater on Thirteenth Avenue and the Holy Cross Bowling Alley on Seventeenth and Fifth Streets.

I had many new duties once I moved to the city. My mother often asked me to go to the store just before dinnertime. Steve Wasik's store was only a half block away on Grand Street, so I could slip down the alley in less than five minutes. For a grocery store,

the 100-year-old building seemed misleadingly distinguished. Pillars added an elegant touch to the tall building, and I remember that the grey cement railings on the stairs were good for sliding. The front of the business contained both a meat market and a small grocery store, while the owners lived in the back of the building.

Steve and his wife Sophie were warm, generous people, and I always left the store happier than when I came in. Steve was tall with a gentle voice, and Sophie was very graceful and wore her long hair in a bun. She would often be out back watering and caring for her flowers when I arrived. Steve always had a friendly greeting for me. "How is my little Jancia?" he would ask. Jancia (Yencha) is Polish for my name.

I liked visiting the store best when no other customers were around, because Steve would have the time to tell me stories and jokes. Sometimes, he offered me a popsicle or a lollipop. And when I returned pop bottles, Steve trusted me to put them in the storeroom if he happened to be busy. I often wondered if he treated other children so specially. Perhaps, he knew we were poor or, maybe, he was just a kind man.

*Schiller School 2620 NE California St. 1920.*

Just around the corner from Steve's store and down a block on Twenty-seventh Avenue, stood Joe and Bessie's store. "Joe's Big Ten" featured a wider variety of merchandise than Steve's. Customers could even purchase toys. Joe and Bessie were one of the few Jewish families in the neighborhood. An unlikely pair, Joe's bald head had a fringe of thinning, white hair, while Bessie's lavish black hair always looked as if she just stepped out of the beauty shop. Joe spoke with a Polish accent, but Bessie's English was meticulous. She dressed fancy with rhinestone glasses that hung on a chain around her neck. But Joe always wore a blood-stained apron, and Bessie often complained that he looked sloppy.

Joe treated me special, too.

"That's Mary's daughter," he often declared to his other patrons in my presence. This remark filled me with pride, and even as a child, I felt I must behave in a proper manner.

"Don't worry, I'll charge the rest on your mother's bill," he would say if I hadn't brought enough money for the groceries. Joe kindly kept a tab for my mother, as he did for many of the other people in the neighborhood. But I'm sure he often neglected to add on the smaller purchases to our bill. If I happened to forget which items my mother sent me to buy, Joe would let me use the phone to call home.

Joe always sent me home with something extra. He would often add another pork chop to our order or invite me to choose a piece of candy from the glass containers lining a shelf behind the counter. For a special treat, Joe would invite me to choose my favorite flavor from the popsicles in the freezer. If I added up all the free candy and popsicles that Joe gave me during those years, I'd probably owe him quite a bit of money.

My mother and my Aunt Vicky did their weekly shopping at Joe and Bessie's on Saturdays. Shopping day was an important event for the two women, and they spent the day combining this household chore with pleasure. They would leave to do their shopping early in the morning before the stores became crowded. After they finished their grocery shopping, Joe would ask my mother and my aunt to join him for a beer and a chat behind the meat counter. If my brother or I happened to be along, we'd be treated to a Coke. Then we'd go home, and a few hours later the groceries would be delivered.

My mother used to send me to the shoemaker on Twenty-second Avenue and Third Street near Bottineau Park. A man named Kus ran the business from the basement of his home. Out of loyalty, my mother insisted upon doing business with him, despite my obvious reluctance to go there, probably because he came from the same village in Poland as my grandparents.

He was a very thin old man, probably in his eighties or nineties, and his hands shook. Kus spoke only Polish, so I had a difficult time trying to convey exactly what I needed. Because he couldn't understand me, I often left with the wrong thing done to a pair of shoes. Naturally, counting change seemed an impossible task for him too. Sometimes, he did the work on the spot while I waited. When he ran the huge sewing machine, his hands shook uncontrollably. The whole situation seemed dangerous, and I was always frightened. Mismatched shoes filled the shop, and Kus continually asked me if I knew who they belonged to.

"These your shoes?" he would ask.

"No," I would repeatedly reply.

"Such waste," he would answer, shaking his head.

Kus always wanted to sell me cleats, explaining in his broken English that my shoes would last longer with them. But cleats made noise, and I did not want people to know we went to the shoemaker, which in my mind would mark my family as being poor.

*My mother's recipe for poppyseed bread.*

## California Street

Most houses on California Street were built of clapboard or stucco with alleys in the backyards and neatly trimmed sidewalks in front. Every house had a screen porch. Vegetable gardens, and flowers and fruit trees flourished in the small yards. Children's shouts and laughter echoed throughout the neighborhood as they walked to school or rode their bikes late into the evenings. Endless games of tag or hopscotch kept children running and hopping, while alleys and empty fields by the railroad tracks served as baseball diamonds.

Residents had common bonds in their backgrounds, so the neighborhoods felt secure and connected. Cousins or sisters often lived on the same block. Neighbors chatted in their native languages across backyard fences and helped one another in any way possible. Just about everyone on our block came from Poland. I remember that whenever our mothers didn't want us kids to understand what they were saying, they spoke Polish.

I heard about the women that gathered for featherplucking parties just like they did in Poland. The feathers would become part of featherbeds and pillows that were passed down through the generations. Often, a bride would receive these heirlooms from her mother or the groom's mother on her wedding day. My mother ordered pillows for each of my sisters as they were married.

The Zembals lived two doors away from our house and invited us to dinner many times. Angela Dziedzic was the grandma and spoke only Polish. She had white hair arranged in soft curls and she always wore

14

*Aerial view of California and Grand Streets, 30th Avenue in the foreground runs left and right. The house on the far right of row of houses directly across from elevator is ours. Photo taken 1910.*

a flowered apron. She loved to have my mother over because they were old friends and had long conversations in Polish. Angela's daughter, Gladys Zembal, helped make my wedding dress and refused to accept money for the many hours of sewing. Her handwork included special details like intricate embroidery and small covered buttons.

Despite the overall residential appearance of our neighborhood, commercial enterprises thrived in our community, too. Grain elevators and industrial buildings dotted the landscape. And at least once every hour, a freight train rumbled through the area. But residents quickly became oblivious to the rhythm and cadence of these sounds. After all, the noises represented prosperity and employment for the neighborhood.

## Soo Line Picnic

My grandfather worked for the Soo Line Railroad as a freight car repairman. Many of my uncles also worked at the Soo Line, as did a great portion of the men living in Northeast Minneapolis. So, naturally the annual Soo Line picnics were greatly appreciated in our neighborhood.

Great anticipation surrounded this annual event. The picnic included a train ride to Annandale, which was quite a wonder in itself. I would join the other kids running the length of the train, drinking all the water, and pestering parents about when we would arrive.

When we finally came to our Annandale destination, our excitement could not be contained. Contests, including relay races, egg tosses, shoe kicks, and raffles, gave everyone a chance to win a prize. But the highlight for my brother and me came with the yo-yo contest. We would practice all summer. Every year I

was eliminated in the first round, but one glorious year my brother actually won an official "Glow-In-The-Dark Duncan Yo-Yo."

## Traditions

My family believed in celebrating the simple pleasures of life. Even though my grandparents were poor, they invited relatives, neighbors, and friends to their house often. My mother continued this tradition after my grandparents died. Parties with polka dancing and live music occurred regularly at the Koniar house. Our neighbor would play the concertina for these events. Cars lined California Street for blocks on party nights. With our large family, a wedding would take place at

*Mr. Iskerka playing the concertina. Mr. Kubinski is in the background doing a traditional dance 1930s.*

least every two years and those celebrations usually lasted several days.

My family celebrated religious holidays with great enthusiasm, too. Preparations began weeks before the day, when my mother started decorating the house. At

Easter, she hid eggs all over the house and in the yard. At Christmas, she hung cards, tinsel, and bells in the living room. Mistletoe and paper cuttings dangled from the chandelier, and a banner with Merry Christmas in big letters adorned the wooden archway between the living room and dining room. On Christmas day, family and friends sang carols around our piano.

Food was an important part of every celebration. My mother purchased special items, such as poppy seed and pig's feet at Kroger's or Sentryz. Huge hams arrived at our house from Joe's Big Ten Store. The aroma of poppy seed bread and sugar donuts filled the house. Among the traditional foods my mother made for celebrations were babka, an iced, braided bread; pig's feet and sauerkraut; Polish sausage; keeshka, better known as blood sausage; golabki, meat and rice wrapped in cabbage; pierogi, a pasta filled with potatoes and cheese; and kluski, small potato dumplings. Sometimes, my mother took the food to church for the priest to bless. Our Christmas Eve Supper always began with the breaking and sharing of the oplatek (blessed wafer in the form of nativity) accompanied by a mutual exchange of wishes.

My mother started another tradition in our family—storytelling. Because we owned only a few school textbooks and Polish prayer books, we took great pleasure in creating our own stories. My mother talked about the old days and her childhood on California Street. She described nickel ice cream cones, and the iceman delivering big blocks of ice right to the door. She spoke about the rag man, who sold bottles and other odds and ends, and how people used to chase him down the alley and try to bargain. My mother told us about how she had been promised in marriage to one of grandpa's boarders who was eighteen years older than she was. She told these stories and many others, over and over. And we joined our mother in this favorite family pastime, adding our memories of holidays and special family events as we sat around the kitchen table late into the night.

At first, I didn't appreciate the significance behind my mother's need to relate the past to her children. But as I matured I began to understand. The past was still vivid in her mind, and she wanted to preserve this rich legacy for her children. Perhaps, she wanted us to appreciate the many comforts we took for granted or, maybe, she felt something vital would be lost forever without her efforts. Whatever reasons she had, I had become her vessel.

My hope is that this book will preserve the memories of a unique place and time in Minneapolis history. A place where people never forgot the heritage of their homelands on the other side of the ocean. And a time when people were grateful for the chance to improve their lives in a new country. A place called Northeast.

*Gramma Koniar talking with the neighbors in our backyard. Mrs. Kayzor in middle and other woman is unknown 1930s.*

*The suspension bridge across the Mississippi River leading into Union Station in Bridge Square on 1st Street North at Hennepin Avenue. The Exposition Building is in the background. It was later bought by M.W. Savage, owner of the famed Dan Patch and eventually became the Coca Cola building site 1888.*

# 2 Northeast Begins as St. Anthony

As the first outpost for soldiers in the Minnesota territory, Fort Snelling offered protection to both travelers and settlers. Just a short distance away from the fort, the roaring waters and scenic beauty of St. Anthony Falls attracted the attention of many artists, writers, politicians, and curious tourists. They came to see for themselves the cataract Father Hennepin and Jonathan Carver had made famous in their books. But the military men who built the fort envisioned a practical use for the falling waters and, subsequently, staked claims near St. Anthony Falls.

The Fort Snelling reserve consisted of about six thousand acres and included the Falls of St. Anthony. Before 1824 it was named Fort St. Anthony. Northeast Minneapolis traces the beginnings of its history to these early days of the falls.

As a result of severe winters, summer droughts, and grasshopper infestations, members of the Selkirk Colony in Canada decided to move south. In 1821, 248 people from the Canadian settlement arrived at Fort Snelling. These people became both the first settlers of St. Anthony Falls and the first agriculturalists to settle in Minnesota. More people joined them when the Red River flooded in 1826.

Among the earliest settlers were many men noted for their enterprising natures. In a modest log cabin, Roswell P. Russell opened the first store in St. Anthony. Pierre Bottineau was a skilled and popular guide for trails in the Northwest territory. William Cheever built an observation deck just south of the present-day University of Minnesota. The sign over his residence read "Pay your dime and climb." Charles Wilson, Joseph Rondo, Samuel Findley, John Rollins, Calvin Tuttle, Luther Patch, Sumner Farnham, Caleb Dorr, Robert Cummings, Charles Stimpson, John McDonald, Samuel Fernald, Joseph and William Marshall, Daniel Stanchfield, and Baptiste Turpin were all men that played key roles in the early settlement of St. Anthony.

On May 10, 1823, the *Virginia* became the first steamboat to successfully navigate the waters of the upper Mississippi. As a result of easier access to the area, St. Anthony Falls became one of the best-known tourist attractions on the North American continent by the mid-1800s.

## Franklin Steele and the Boom Years

President Van Buren appointed 25-year-old Franklin Steele as sutler of Fort Snelling. And when Andrew Jackson added his encouragement, young Steele decided to go to the new territories and make his fortune. Steele became a big investor in the fortune of St. Anthony. He staked a settler's claim to property on the east side of the Mississippi River and began constructing a mess hall, carpentry and blacksmith shops, stables, and a bunkhouse. In 1849, he registered a plat, which included 250 acres of the St. Anthony townsite, Hennepin Island, Boom Island, and frontage on Nicollet Island, as well as water rights, the dam, and the mill.

For St. Anthony, 1847 marked the arrival of many other New Englanders who became influential founders and builders of Minneapolis. Steele hired Ard Godfrey, a friend from Maine, to build the first privately-owned sawmill in the city. From the very first lumber sawed in this mill in 1849, Godfrey erected a one-and-a-half story, classic Greek Revival house, which remains the oldest house in Minneapolis.

By 1850, 538 people resided in St. Anthony. According to a 1850 census about fifty percent of the men found employment as either lumbermen or laborers, while a smaller percentage worked as carpenters and farmers. Two-thirds of the new arrivals came from northeastern states, and over half of those settlers hailed from Maine. Fewer commercial and agricultural opportunities in New England led to this influx of families from that part of the country. Also, many New Englanders were recruited because of their expertise in the lumbering industry. Other significant proportions of newcomers arrived from Ireland and Canada.

Evolving from a collection of makeshift shanties, Steele's village rapidly took on the appearance of a thriving town. Anson Northrup erected the St. Charles Hotel on Marshall Street and Sixth Avenue in 1850.

The two-story building, large for the period, could accommodate seventy-five guests. The hotel provided a ballroom for dancing, and soon became the social center of the village. By December of 1851, *The St. Anthony Express* reported that 1400 people resided in the city. Two stage lines competed keenly for business and two schools opened, one of which overlooked the falls from a prairie bluff. A library association incorporated and purchased 200 volumes for the community. In 1854, Steele built the first suspension bridge across the Mississippi River. This bridge connected the two growing communities on the east and west banks of the Mississippi River.

In 1855, St. Anthony was incorporated as a city. Standard size lots for houses were a quarter acre of land, while streets were eighty feet wide, except Main Street, which was 100 feet wide. Ard Godfrey served as postmaster in the newly established post office. Gardens and picket fences surrounded the white houses. Stagecoaches arrived from St. Paul bringing settlers from New England, Canada, and the South. The noise from the sawmills could be heard above the falls. The First Universalist Society of St. Anthony dedicated a church in 1857 that stands today as the oldest continuously used church in Minneapolis.

Originally, Steele's vision for St. Anthony included multiple civic structures and the newly forming University of Minnesota. However, by 1856 his financial and legal affairs were in such a shambles that the University regents voted to abandon the idea of building in St. Anthony and decided to relocate the fledgling college downstream at the site of the present campus.

*Anson Northrup's Tavern of the first St.Charles Hotel. Marshall Street NE and Wood Street (6th Avenue) 1849. Visitors could view the falls from the upper Piazza then take the ten minute walk to the steamboat wharf. It was later destroyed by fire.*

## Early Settlement of Minneapolis

The land across the Mississippi River from St. Anthony opened to settlers for purchase in 1855, and 20,661 acres on the west bank sold at a minimum price of $1.25 per acre. The population increased to 1,555 at the end of 1856. Throughout these early years milling remained a key factor in the community's economy. The mills on the west side had been consolidated into a partnership of twelve men who formed the Minneapolis Mill Company in 1856. The west side village at first looked to St. Anthony for leadership and very little rivalry existed between the settlements. In most circumstances, the two communities united against their rival down the river—St. Paul.

## St. Anthony Becomes the East Side of Minneapolis

Two main business districts existed in the fledgling community of St. Anthony. The extensive sawmills of Lower Town supplied St. Paul and the surrounding country with lumber, and the settlement near the steamboat landing opposite the northern end of Nicollet Island became known as Upper Town.

People from Maine tended to settle in Lower Town, while several ethnic groups chose to live in the Upper Town section. Consequently, marked differences existed between the two areas. The Maine settlement contained no drinking establishments.

The vicinity of the upper levee along Main Street seemed destined in the early days to be the Wall Street of the future city. D.B. Dorman erected a hand-some brick block at the corner of Broadway and Jackson Streets which included the Dorman Bank, Nash's Hardware and Mills' General Store. Wensinger opened a shoe store in 1849 and four dry goods stores existed along Main Street. At a later date, Henry Webber and

*Weber Grocery Store, 604 Marshall St., 1910.*

Hamlin, Holmes and Hollister and Sam Stanchfield opened grocery and notion stores. The first ten-pin alley in St. Anthony, owned by Alex Cloutier was opened just north of the bank building. The Alhambra Saloon and Father Kline's Place, known for good lager beer were favorite gathering places.

The pride of Lower Town was a row of saw mills located on the St. Anthony Falls dam. This area also boasted two substantial business blocks that ran from Second to Fourth Avenues along Southeast Main Street, the Upton and Morrison/Martin Blocks. Not far downstream were Bernard Brothers Furniture, Barton General Store, Bantley Bakery, and Rogers, Stanton and Keaton Sash and Door Manufacturing. In the summer of 1849, the first public school was opened in a small log shanty near Second Street by Miss Electra Backus. The "Little Black School House" was so-called because it was unpainted and dulled in tone by sun and rain.

The fortunes of the two water power companies reversed the positions of the newly forming village on the west bank of the Mississippi, soon to be named Minneapolis, and St. Anthony. Mismanagement and the nationwide Panic of 1857, paralyzed key St. Anthony financial institutions and halted immigration to the area. Steele, one of the most influential men in St. Anthony, lost his New York benefactor, John Sanford. Subsequently, New York investments were abruptly suspended. After thirteen years of lawsuits and fighting to save his company, Steele quietly relinquished his post.

The St. Anthony Water Power Company was

*Pioneer Square statue 5th and Marshall St. moved from Gateway Center.*

threatened with auction to pay debts and the newly established manufacturing firm created by the power company did not provide enough employment or money to spur the growth of St. Anthony. By 1869, the village on the west bank of the Mississippi was producing five times the flour and two times the lumber as the town of St. Anthony.

Because of the twin manufacturing districts, maintenance of the two separate but duplicate economies seemed a needless and wasteful draw on limited resources. Discussions about a merger between the two towns began as early as the 1850s. However, combining the east and west bank became urgent business in

*St. Anthony Pottery, 810 Marshall St., about 1897.*

*First house built on Grand Street in 1865 by Walter Walsh at 1317 Grand.*

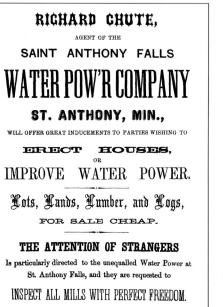

RICHARD CHUTE,

AGENT OF THE

SAINT ANTHONY FALLS

# WATER POW'R COMPANY

ST. ANTHONY, MIN.,

WILL OFFER GREAT INDUCEMENTS TO PARTIES WISHING TO

**ERECT HOUSES,**

OR

IMPROVE WATER POWER.

Lots, Lands, Lumber, and Logs,

FOR SALE CHEAP.

**THE ATTENTION OF STRANGERS**

Is particularly directed to the unequalled Water Power at St. Anthony Falls, and they are requested to

INSPECT ALL MILLS WITH PERFECT FREEDOM.

*1860 City Directory advertisement of lots.*

*John Ingehutt, Great Grandfather of Harriet Reiners Leitschuh about 1912, 29th-30th and Marshall St. where NSP now stands (faced east). Later became potatoe farms.*

the 1860s with St. Paul leading in population and its importance in navigation increasing every year. Minneapolis incorporated as a city in 1867, and the new city's influence and power eventually overshadowed St. Anthony.

Eventually, St. Anthony became the East Side of Minneapolis. After merging with Minneapolis in 1872, St. Anthony looked to this westerly neighbor for employment and recreation. During this time, the East Hennepin-Central Avenue triangle evolved into the major business center of the East Side.

## The Early East Side Community

The city of Minneapolis continued to grow at a rapid pace. In 1871, the establishment of Minneapolis Gas Light Company and a city sewer system both hinted at the needs of a rapidly expanding population. The

*Group of Northeast men building the Soo Line Railroad about 1900.*

Northwest Telephone Exchange Company installed two hundred telephones by 1878 and the Minnesota Brush Electric Company built the first hydroelectric station in the United States and began lighting the city in 1883. In the 1880s, cement and artificial stone sidewalks slowly began to replace wooden ones. By 1895, paved streets accounted for over twenty-five miles of roadway. Cedar block paved most streets, but granite was used where traffic was heaviest.

The St. Anthony portion provided its share of commercial growth to the new Minneapolis community. Constructed in 1880, the East Side Pillsbury Elevator marked the site where the Steele-Godfrey grist mill first began operation in 1851. Located between First and Second Streets Southeast, the new Pillsbury Mill was seven stories high with the capacity of producing 4,000 barrels a day and, for a time, led the world in flour production.

The East District had three fire companies that totaled about 150 men: the Cataract Engine Company on Third Avenue Southeast Main Street; the Minnesota Engine Company on Fifth Avenue between Main and Marshall Streets; and the Germania Engine Company on Thirteenth and Second Street. In 1885, firemen began to respond to calls from the 18 fire boxes on the East Side with a horse-drawn wagon carrying 650 feet of hose and a Babcock extinguisher.

The East Side Pumping Station opened in 1885 and gave the community an independent source of water. Heavy traffic from Orth's Brewery prompted the installation on Thirteenth Avenue and Marshall Street of one of the earliest street lamps. The Great Minneapolis Exposition opened in the newly constructed Exposition Building in 1885, and the only Republican

*Engine Co. #2 of the Main Street Fire Department near 13th Avenue NE 1909.*

national convention Minnesota has ever hosted took place in that structure in 1892. The building eventually became a Coca-Cola bottling plant. The first East Side electric car began a short run on Central Avenue in 1891. In the same year, a Second Street Line and a Monroe Line also started limited runs. A neighborhood newspaper, *The Northeast Argus*, issued its first edition in 1891.

Division Street, later renamed East Hennepin Avenue, marked the boundary between the Northeast and Southeast sections of Minneapolis. The Southeast sector of the city prospered quite early. Because the Pillsbury clan settled close to the family mill on the Southeast side, other entrepreneurs followed their example. And, of course, the Southeast side constantly benefited from the presence of the University of Minnesota. The needs of a continually burgeoning faculty, student population, and staff guaranteed consistent growth even in troubled economic times.

*Gluek Brewing Co. keg wagon drawn by pure-bred Belgian mares, bred and raised on the Gluek Farms 1930.*

Meanwhile, the manufacturing and railroad industries expanded in Northeast Minneapolis. The Soo Line Railroad, under the direction of Thomas Lowry, established extensive railyards in Northeast. Brewing also became a significant enterprise. And in 1880, the Minneapolis Brewing and Malting Company incorporated four older companies: Germania, Heinrich, Noerenberg, and Orth. Later renamed the Grain Belt Brewery, this company and the Gluek Company provided employment for and quenched the thirsts of the working population of Northeast for several decades.

In the late nineteenth century, Central Avenue had a primarily commercial and industrial character. This street connected the vast railway networks spanning Broadway Avenue and linked Minneapolis with the smaller towns to the north. At the juncture of Central Avenue and Lowry Avenue Northeast, a community known as New Boston flourished. Henry B. Beard, an early developer, constructed over 100 houses along the wide New Boston avenues between 1885 and 1892. He also created the commercial center on Central Avenue between Twenty-fourth and Twenty-fifth Avenues. This area later became known as the Elmwood area because of the many elm trees the city planted along its streets.

On the land sloping down to the riverside between Marshall Street and the Mississippi River, another residential district became the first American neighborhood for many immigrants. Poles and other Slavic groups first settled in Northeast in this low-lying area called " the Flats" on the Mississippi's east bank opposite Nicollet and Boom Islands. In the Flats, the newly arriving immigrants could find affordable housing in the two and three story buildings that served as rudimentary hotels. The long rectangular structures consisted of many small rooms, and these bedrooms often had no windows because the buildings had common walls. In some cases, owners rented the rooms using the hot bed system, where customers paid for lodgings only during the hours they needed to sleep.

Northeast housed immigrants during various stages of their climb up the American ladder. Central Avenue was the unofficial boundary between the families just arriving, and the families more firmly established and prosperous. Moving from the valley neighborhoods of Old St. Anthony and Sheridan to the hill communities of Windom Park and Audubon Park confirmed a family's upwardly mobile social and economic status. The dilapidated shacks of the Flats contrasted sharply with the tidy frame houses and duplexes in the hill communities. Valley children walked to school, while children from the hill areas rode to school on the streetcars, confirming their higher positions. But the old timers living close to the river insisted that "the valley people" were the real "Nordeasters."

*The first frame house in St. Anthony, built by R.P. Russel in 1848. Pierre Bottineau cut the logs and floated them down to the mill. House once stood on upper side of North Main, on the Great Northern Railroad tracks. 115-3rd Avenue NE.*

Distinct ethnic neighborhoods developed largely as a result of the timing and talents associated with the great waves of immigration. French, Scandinavian, Irish and German immigrants arrived in St. Anthony in the mid-1800s. By the late 1800s and early 1900s, the second wave hit Northeast, bringing Poles, Slovaks, and Ukrainians from the Carpathian Mountain area bordering Poland and Czechoslovakia. These groups often left their villages because of overpopulation and poverty, and arrived in America with few skills and unable to speak English. Lying alongside the Mississippi and adjacent to railroad yards, as well as lumber and flour mills, Northeast quickly acquired an industrial character which suited these immigrants and their needs.

Another wave of immigration came after World War II, when more eastern Europeans and Lebanese[*] escaped the hardships and war in their own countries by fleeing to America. They added their languages, their customs, and their religions to the already diverse Northeast atmosphere.

Divided by railroad tracks and industrial districts, Northeast eventually consisted of twenty to thirty distinct communities representing different cultures. Germans tended to congregate along Broadway Avenue near the Grain Belt Brewery. Fourth Street became "Russian Boulevard". The area just east of University Avenue and south of Thirty-seventh Avenue was known as "Little Moscow." Swedes, then Italians, congregated near Maple Hill, later called Beltrami. Main street for the Nordic immigrant was referred to as "Swede Alley." Thirty-first and Fillmore became "Norwegian Hill" The north side of Broadway was "New Boston" and the south side was known as "Dogtown" to residents. The Poles chose Thirteenth and University Avenues as their downtown and called the area "Little Poland" or "Little Warsaw." Ukrainians chose the area around Harrison Street and Broadway Avenue. Slovaks settled on Thirteenth Avenue and Third Street, while pockets of Latvians, Estonians, Lebanese and Armenians could be found in old St. Anthony near Main and Marshall Streets.

Even today, families from the same European town often occupy the same block in Northeast Minneapolis. There are still neighborhoods where Polish or Russian is commonly spoken, and children often live in the homes their grandparents built. This ethnic solidarity plus strong religious and social ties keep second and third generation families from leaving the Northeast area for the suburbs. The legacy of their forebears remains embedded in the architecture, the neighborhoods, the businesses, and—most of all—the history of Northeast Minneapolis.

[*] Note. There is a legend that the lower Northeast area down by the river has always been safe and protected from strong winds because when Fr. Hennepin came down the river he blessed that area.

*St. Anthony Chapel built in 1851.*

# 3 A Church on Every Corner

By Nancy S. Doerfler

More than any other institution, the churches of Northeast Minneapolis reflect the rich heritage and diversity of Northeast's ethnic communities. By tracing the history of the churches, the soul of this unique community emerges. In turn, eight major ethnic groups settled in Northeast Minneapolis and built churches in their newly adopted neighborhoods. The French, Germans, Swedes, Slovaks, Italians, Polish, East Slavs, and the Lebanese clustered around their national churches, which symbolized and preserved the traditions of the Old World. As a result, Northeast Minneapolis has a church on almost every corner, and over a dozen of these churches are still closely associated with their founding ethnic communities.

## ST. ANTHONY OF PADUA

*The Stations of the Cross at the Church of St. Anthony of Padua depict the crucifixion of Jesus with vivid colors accentuating the crown of thorns, blood, and eyes of Jesus. Each station is mounted on a shelf supported by two cherub angels. These stations have become a rare form of liturgical art dating back to the turn of the century.*

The earliest white settlers to Northeast Minneapolis were French Canadians from the Red River settlement near the Canadian border. Among these new settlers were many Metis, people of both Native American and French Canadian lineage. As trappers and traders, the Metis became familiar with the area around Fort Snelling when traveling to the area to sell their furs and buy provisions. With the decline of the fur trade and poor harvests, a steadily increasing number of these settlers moved to the area around the Falls of St. Anthony. By 1847, a community of over fifty French Canadians lived in sod and elm bark huts along the Mississippi.

As a voyager, interpreter, and guide to governors and generals, Pierre Bottineau became one of the most illustrious Metis. Like most of his fellow French Canadians, Bottineau was Catholic. In 1849, Bottineau donated fourteen lots for a church, which he named St. Anthony of Padua after the falls.

One of two French priests sent to the St. Paul settlement in the early 1840s, Father Augustin Ravoux first served the Native American missions. As the Catholic settlers at St. Anthony increased, Ravoux felt the worshipers needed a chapel. In 1849, Ravoux began building a frame and log structure that became the first church in Minneapolis. With the help of Bottineau and other French Canadians, namely, the Cloutier, Poncin, Crepan, Huit, Boutin, Gervais, LeCount, Potvin, Moran and Raiche families, Ravoux dedicated the church in 1851.

The French order of Sisters of St. Joseph established the first parochial school in the state in 1853. The curriculum included Latin, music and English. In 1851, Father Denis Ledon began serving as pastor of St. Anthony. St. Mary's convent and boarding school were completed in 1855. Thirty of the eighty students attending the school lived at the convent. Tuition was fifty cents a month but free to the poorer students.

*First St. Anthony High School Graduating Class 1885. Annie Bohan (Walsh) Dolly Fleetham (Hoy) and Mary Jarrett (Sister Josepha).*

As the parish attracted ever-increasing numbers of Catholics to St. Anthony, the church soon became too small. Father John Fayolle, a native of France, succeeded Ledon in 1857 and began construction of a larger church. Bottineau donated the land for this church, also.

During the pastorate of Fayolle, the ethnic mix of the parish shifted. The late 1850s and 1860s brought immigrants from Ireland and Germany, as well as many New England settlers. The French Canadians no longer dominated the community. With diverse languages and customs, groups clashed as each attempted to preserve its own culture. Fayolle wrote in 1858:

"We have to meet with various nationalities having each of their own ideas, manners and prejudices. One must exercise much control over oneself in order to deal with usages which differ from those to which one is accustomed, and then there still remains the difficult task of establishing peace among everyone, especially between Irish, Canadians and Germans. The prejudices of race are very strong and seldom yield to reason. The Irish would like an Irish priest, the Germans, a German and so on, a thing which is quite impossible to do."

German Catholics formed their own church within St. Anthony's borders in 1857, which they named St. Boniface. With so many parishioners leaving, funding for St. Anthony declined drastically and, by 1860, the school closed. The sisters returned to their convent in St. Paul, and Fayolle's health declined.

Father John McDermott, an Irishman, replaced Fayolle as St. Anthony's pastor in 1860. Under his guidance, parishioners completed the second church and reopened the school. As even more settlers came under his care, McDermott acquired land for a new stone church and school. In June of 1862, Bishop Thomas Grace gave the sacrament of confirmation to the first class of ninety-four parishioners.

When McDermott transferred in 1866, Father Felix Tissot succeeded him and finished the new stone church and school. The return of a French pastor did not ease tensions between the French and Irish parishioners. Baptismal and marriage records for 1877 indicate the parish consisted of a nearly equal number of French and Irish residents.

The French Catholics resolved to worship in their native language and left St. Anthony in July of 1877 to establish Our Lady of Lourdes. Within eighteen

*St. Mary's Convent 1854–1888.*

months of the French departure ten of the eleven marriages recorded occurred between people of Irish descent. And with the appointment in 1886 of Father James O'Reilly, followed by Father Patrick Kenny, any parish ties to the French community disappeared. St. Anthony had become an Irish church.

## OUR LADY OF LOURDES

*The fleur-de-lis, a cross and lily symbolizing the resurrection of Jesus, appears on the doors and carpets at Our Lady of Lourdes Church. Members of the First Universalist Society presented the Kneeling Angel baptismal font to the parish in 1971. It is the only known copy of Thorwaldsen's Kneeling Angel, which was created in Rome in 1827. T. Stein carved the font in Copenhagen in 1891.*

When the Universalist Church became available, the French parishioners of St. Anthony of Padua, led by Leandre Gagnon and Joseph Rivet, purchased the building for $5,000. Constructed in 1857 on Prince Street, the church was in the ideal location for the French population. Father Pascal Brunnelle became pastor of the new church, which the members named Our Lady of Lourdes. Parishioners celebrated the first Mass in the former Universalist Church on July 29, 1877.

Father Z. L. Chandonnet, the second pastor, enlarged the limestone church in 1880. Originally a rectangular Greek-style building, the effect of the renovations was reminiscent of the Gothic architecture of French European cathedrals. For the next decade, the parish and its surrounding communities flourished as an economic depression in Canada resulted in a steady flow of French immigrants.

## ST. BONIFACE

*A huge arched window in the Church of St. Boniface describes the life of this saint and was crafted in the 1930s. Three square windows below the Boniface window depict Monte Cassino, the Abbey of Mettin, and St. John's Abbey, which honor the Benedictine connections of this church. The plaster arch surrounding the altar also displays the Benedictine symbols of the heart, the Blessed Virgin Mary, the Alpha and Omega, and the Benedictine cross.*

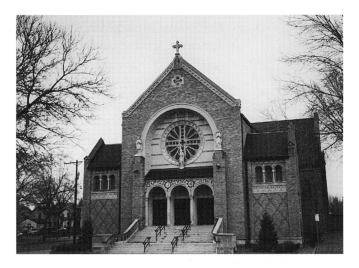

In the 1850s, the German Father Francis Pierz wrote a letter to entice his fellow countrymen in Milwaukee, Cincinnati, and even across the ocean, to move to the western territories.

"Come to the beautiful state of Minnesota," he wrote. "You will in a short time be able to obtain very valuable land of beautiful meadows of the best soil."

These words proved especially powerful to the people of Germany. German unification had resulted in political unrest and religious persecution. Because the iron controls of the government altered the economic balance, shop owners and merchants found the new industrial-military society unfriendly to commerce. The lure of a fertile new land and prosperous enterprises across the sea proved a great attraction. Germans began to arrive in Minnesota in substantial numbers by 1855. As businessmen, not farmers or laborers like many immigrant groups, the Germans came with funds to start commercial ventures, such as banks, grocery stores, breweries, or saloons.

In 1856, German Jesuit Father Francis X. Weninger conducted a mission in St. Paul at Assumption Church. The German Catholics, who regularly worshiped at St. Anthony of Padua with French priests, asked Weninger to help them establish a parish for the Germans. In October of that year, Weninger met with St. Anthony's German Catholics, and a group of thirteen people became charter members of the new church. This group included Valentine and Carl Kaeg, as well as the Hubert Brooks, Philip Pick, and Peter Weingarten families. Charter member Bartholomew Ganzer donated two lots on the northeast corner of Fifteenth Avenue and Third Street for the church.

Father Weninger suggested St. Boniface, apostle to the Germans, for the patron saint of the new church, and building commenced in 1857. But that year was one of financial crisis across the region, and construction of the church halted. Work on the structure resumed the next year, and workers finished building by August of 1859. Father Eberhardt Gahr, assistant pastor at Assumption, accepted an appointment to the German mission church.

The German immigrants considered a school vital to preserve their heritage. They established St. Boniface School in 1875 and asked the Sisters of Christian Charity to teach. Work on a new church and the school began in 1899. Because the new church was built in stages, parishioners attended Mass in the basement of the church, which was known as "the catacombs." Members laid the cornerstone for the present church in 1929.

*Zenith Dramatic Club Production 1935.*

## EMANUEL EVANGELICAL LUTHERAN CHURCH

*Shipbuilders by trade, the creators of the Emanuel Evangelical Lutheran Church modeled the interior after the deck of a ship. A huge oil painting of Jesus, Mary and Martha depicting Jesus' journey to Bethany before the crucifixion hangs in the sanctuary.*

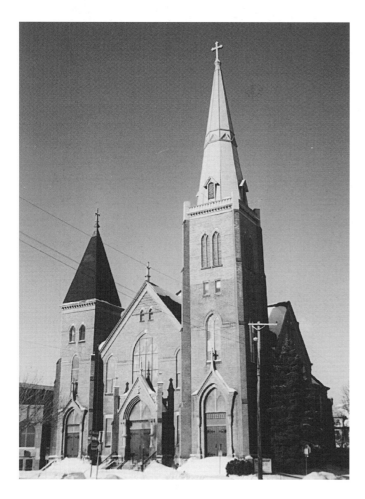

Unlike many other immigrant groups, desperate economic conditions in their homeland were not the motivation causing the first Swedes to arrive in Minnesota in the 1850s. Also different than the many previous waves of migration that involved mostly single male laborers, the Swedish migration consisted of families. These rural people searching for affordable farmland found fertile soil in the Chisago Lake area.

In 1868–69, a severe crop failure and widespread hunger in Sweden compelled a second wave of Swedes to emigrate. These immigrants were mostly young, single people. Swedish men found employment in the sawmills, flour mills, and breweries of Northeast Minneapolis. Young women became domestic servants or worked in dressmaking or millinery shops. Naturally, the growing city created an increasing demand for any who were skilled craftsmen, such as stone cutters, blacksmiths, tailors and bricklayers.

Most Swedish immigrants practiced the Lutheran faith and, upon their arrival, joined the established Swedish churches in south Minneapolis. But by 1872, rather than walk the long distance across the river to worship, the Lutherans of Northeast Minneapolis started a Sunday school on their side of the river. In 1884, the congregation of thirty-one charter members organized the Emanuel Evangelical Lutheran Church. And in 1892, the parishioners of Emanuel purchased land at Thirteenth Avenue and Monroe Street Northeast for a church and began to build. Families celebrated the first service in the new sanctuary in 1899.

Eventually, almost every Swedish citizen had a

relative or friend in America whose letters described higher wages and growing prosperity. This correspondence inspired a steady immigration, particularly from young men in farming families searching for greater opportunities. By the 1900s, Fifth Street marked the boundary between the Scandinavian, Ukrainian, and Polish neighborhoods. The Scandinavians lived to the east, while the majority of the Ukrainians and Poles resided on the west side of Fifth Street.

Front Row #1    Middle #2    Class of 1930    Back #3
1-6              1-10                          1-8

--Eunice Madeline Anderson Holstrom        --Ralph Elmer Johnson
3-}Edith Florence Benson                    --Harold John Johnson
--Lawrence O. Bonander                      --Clarence M. E. Linden
--Ralph Howard Bolmgren                     --Harriet Martina Johnson
--Esther Amy Bjorkman                       --Nina Inga Nelson
--Ruth Irene Bjorkman                       --Ethel H. Graff
--Walter John Bjorkman                      --Theodore Edmund Olson
--Orville Harlan Carlson                    --Florence Eleanore Pearson
--Ellen Ingrid Carlson                      --Gordon Thomas Simonson
--Ruth Evaline Carlson Dechaine             --Ruth Allene Smith Howard
--Esther Bertha Carlen                      --Lois Marie Smith
--George Douglas Goble                      --Geneva Inotte Stendahl

*Confirmation Class of 1930.*

37

## ELIM SWEDISH BAPTIST CHURCH

*In the Elim Swedish Baptist Church, the "Elim" memorial window refers to the people's escape from Egypt in the bible. Symbolizing a place of rest after crisis, the Elim of the bible offered the weary journeyers both shade and water. "And they came to Elim where there were twelve springs and seventy palm trees and they camped there beside the springs." (Exodus 15:27)*

Not all Swedes were Lutheran, and religious conflicts weighed heavily in the decision of these Swedish citizens to leave their birthplace. In the mid-1800s, many Swedes joined the Baptist and Methodist churches. The state Swedish Lutheran Church considered these religions heretical and state officials deemed private religious gatherings involving these faiths illegal and punishable by fine or prison. As a result, many practicing Baptists and Methodists decided to emigrate. As early as 1884, Swedish Baptists attended service at Bethlehem Church in Minneapolis. Transportation problems motivated the Northeast congregation to es-

tablish its own community. A Swedish sewing society began in 1884 at the home of the John Halvorsons on Jefferson Street. This group became the Ebenezer Society and, later, the Elim Mission Society. Members met in two rooms of the Northeast Baptist Church on Madison Street and Thirteenth Avenue Northeast. Parishioners also organized a Sunday school, which met in borrowed facilities.

By 1888, the community wanted their own church and pastor. Led by Dr. Frank Peterson, members organized Elim Swedish Baptist Church and purchased two lots on the corner of Twentieth and Jackson Streets Northeast. Building began under the pastorate of Rev. Peter Ostrom. Later, parishioners built a new church at 685 Thirteenth Avenue Northeast.

After the Second World War, the Swedish presence in the area lessened as many families moved to south Minneapolis or the suburbs. Only the area east of Fillmore Street and north of Eighteenth Avenue continued to be identified as the Swedish section of Northeast Minneapolis.

# HOLY CROSS CHURCH

*Since the year 1200 in France, basilicas and cathedrals have featured rose windows similar to the one in Holy Cross Church. The discordant colors and patterns on rose windows depict the chaos of the world, whereas the surrounding circle represents God's order embracing the turmoil. According to Polish legend, a vandal slashed the original painting of Our Lady of Czestochowa and was struck dead. Later, when the shrine was destroyed by fire, only the painting could be salvaged. However, the smoke and flames darkened the image and, henceforth, the painting has been called* The Black Madonna. *The painting in Holy Cross is a reproduction donated by the Polish White Eagle Association.*

Although the first immigrants from Poland settled in Minnesota in 1855, the 1870s mark a significant increase in immigration. Emancipation of peasant serfs, consolidation of small land holdings into large farms, and modernization of agriculture dislocated farm workers in great numbers. A new industrial economy developed, and unskilled rural laborers could not find jobs. With the population throughout Poland doubling in regions like Galacia from 1850 to 1910, even the improved agricultural methods did not satisfy the rising demand for food. Additionally, Russia, Prussia, and Austria divided Poland's lands at various points from 1795 to 1905. These governments barred the Polish language from schools, public gatherings, and even casual meetings. The physical, economic, and ethnic constraints provoked steady migration from Poland.

The first Polish settlers arrived in Northeast Minneapolis in the late 1860s. Original pioneers included the Jarosz, Rapacz and Miskowicz families from Rapka. The Wiscenewski, Sokol, Sledz, Katzmarek, and Ostrovoc families followed soon thereafter. The majority of Poles settling in Northeast came from the Galacia region in Austrian-controlled Poland. Many of them from the villages of Rabka, Jordanow and the town of Nowy Tag in Podhale, the foothills of the Carpathians. Galacia represented the poorest and least industrialized, but most culturally free area of the country.

The Poles shared a profound faith, devotion to their language, and a nostalgia for their native land. A crucifix hewn of wood and a clod of earth from the village of their birth often served as their only keepsakes from the old country. Upon their arrival, the immigrants lived in boarding houses or with other families until they could build homes of their own. The Polish neighborhood extended from Fifth Avenue to Broadway Avenue and from Sibley Street near the Mississippi River to Marshall Street in an area known as the Flats. As the immigrants could afford better housing, they moved from the Flats to the neighborhoods between Second and Sixth Streets.

A visit to Frank Lilla's store at 907 University Northeast or Louis Brzezinski's store at Ninth Avenue and Fourth Street resulted not only in the purchase of food but news about the changing conditions in Europe as well as the fate of Polish immigrants throughout America. And as owners of these informal bureaus of information, the stores' proprietors read and wrote letters for their customers.

The Catholic Polish families first worshiped at the St. Boniface Church or St. Anthony of Padua. However, many Polish immigrants traveled to St. Adalbert's in St. Paul for confession or just to hear a sermon in their native language.

In 1884, John Ziemkowski, Frank Lilla, and Boleslaus Volkman organized a committee headed by St. Adalbert's pastor, Father Dominic Mager, to ask Bishop Ireland to establish a Polish parish. The bishop approved the request. To symbolize their devout faith in the face of the difficult fortunes of the Polish nation, members chose the name Holy Cross for the new parish. They purchased two lots on the southeast corner of Seventeenth Avenue and Fourth Street Northeast, and the bishop invited a Polish-born student studying for the priesthood at the American College in Belgium to the diocese. Seminarian James Pacholski finished his studies in St.

*First Communion of Vicki Koniar (My aunt) attendants are Pauline Wolinski, Wanda Wolinski and Rose Swede.*

Paul and became Holy Cross' first pastor after his ordination in 1886.

For their first church, Holy Cross parishioners bought the original 1851 St. Anthony of Padua building for $25 and moved it to the Fourth Street Northeast property in 1886. The following year, members arranged for the construction of a rectory, and Holy Cross School opened with an enrollment of forty pupils during 1888 in a four-room house behind the church.

When Bishop Ireland noted the overflowing crowd at a confirmation service in 1891, he suggested the parish build a larger church. The following year, construction began on a new brick church capable of seating 500 people. Father Henry Jajeski, another native of Poland, succeeded Father Pacholski in 1894. Under his leadership, members built a convent in 1901 followed by a school in 1906. The third Holy Cross Church, built in 1928, still stands at Seventeenth Street and University Avenue and is the largest Polish parish west of Chicago.

Folk songs, dance and music are woven into the Polish culture, with the most important instrument being the violin. The Poles also share a rich food tradition. Each year on the Thursday before lent, paczki day is observed at Holy Cross. Paczki (fruit-filled doughnuts) are served, symbolizing the final outbreaks of feasting and merry making before the onset of a seven week long fast. Polish folk art includes beautifully painted wooden chests, tables and benches, glass painting, intricate doilies and lacework, designed metal work, hand-carved Swiatki (wooden religious figures), and superb paper cuttings called Wycinanki.

In 1914, conflicts over parish affairs led a group of Polish Catholics to leave Holy Cross Parish and form Sacred Heart Polish National Church at 2200 Fifth Street Northeast with Reverend Klos as the first pastor. In that same year, Holy Cross' assistant priest, Father Maximilian Klesmit, became pastor of a newly established St. Hedwig's Parish. At first, members of St. Hedwig's used the Holy Cross auditorium for Mass. But in 1915, St. Hedwig's parishioners purchased the old church of St. Clement and moved the structure to Twenty-ninth Avenue and Grand Street. In 1919, a new church building was erected, and a school opened under the guidance of the Sisters of St. Francis.

A fourth parish for the Polish people, All Saints, organized in 1916. Members worshiped at Our Lady of Mount Carmel until Father Francis Matz led a successful effort to build both a church and school at 435 Northeast Fourth Street in 1918. In 1938, a larger Romanesque style church replaced the 1918 building.

## OUR LADY OF MOUNT CARMEL

*Our Lady of Mount Carmel Church confirms the Italian community's devotion to the Blessed Virgin. A statue from Italy depicts Mary holding the Christ child and wearing the lighted crown typical of Eastern European statues. A brown scapular in her hand symbolizes the influence of Benedictine monks.*

Italian artisans and merchants began arriving in Minnesota in the 1850s. Noted for their mosaic tile and terrazzo work, the artisans worked on many of the first Minnesota churches and commercial buildings. Italian merchants sold fruit and vegetables from carts, stands, or stores.

By the late nineteenth century, conditions in Italy motivated even larger numbers of Italian citizens to emigrate. Italy's population doubled from 1861 to 1936, and these growing families reduced individual land holdings to "fazzoletti" or property the size of handkerchiefs. With oppressive taxes, poor soil, recurring drought, malaria epidemics, and exploitative landlords compounding the already bleak situation, many Italians decided to search for better opportunities elsewhere.

When these immigrants arrived in America, they maintained their strong family ties and ethnic attributes. Families often lived communally with extended family members. Flourishing gardens and barnyard animals supplemented their diets. Known for their wine-making, oral traditions, folk tales, and infectious humor, the Italians of Northeast Minneapolis worked in section gangs or in the shops of the Soo Line Railroad. In time, many Italian workers also secured positions in the Pillsbury flour mills.

By the 1880s, Italian men began to replace Irish and Scandinavian males as railroad workers on the Great Northern and Northern Pacific crews. Railroads recruited tens of thousands of men each year and transported them from Chicago to "railroad frontiers" in Wisconsin, Minnesota, and Iowa.

In 1907, a chapel for the Italians opened the annex of the Immaculate Conception Church, later to become the Basilica of St. Mary. In this small, dark room, Father R. Balducci from the St. Paul Seminary offered Mass to his Italian parishioners. A few years later, Pastor A. B. Bandini purchased the old German Lutheran church at Main Street and Seventh Avenue for the Italian parish. Members dedicated the $5,500 building to Our Lady of Mount Carmel in 1910. Over one hun-

*Members of the congregation carry a statue of Our Lady of Mount Carmel during the church's celebration of its 50th anniversary July 17th, 1988. About 100 people participated in a procession that went throuh Beltrami Park and through the streets of the Italian neighborhood.*

dred families worshiped at this site until 1919. The location proved inconvenient and, eventually, Syrian Maronites bought the building.

For the next twenty years, Italians did not have their own church. Instead, they attended services at the Margaret Barry Settlement House in Maple Hill. But in 1938, church members purchased the second church of Our Lady of Mount Carmel at Summer and Fillmore Streets. Located in the heart of Minneapolis' Little Italy, this site quickly became the focus of Italian social and religious life. Until World War II, the Italian feast day celebrations constituted some of the most colorful events of the year in Northeast Minneapolis.

The Italians of the Maple Hill neighborhood represented groups from the Mezzogiorno, Calabria, and Abruzzi regions of Italy. Maple Hill, renamed Beltrami in 1948, remained a vital Italian community until after World War II. With its own school, church, settlement house, and independent businesses, the neighborhood was completely self-sufficient until Highway 35W divided the area in the 1960s and scattered the families of many of the original immigrants.

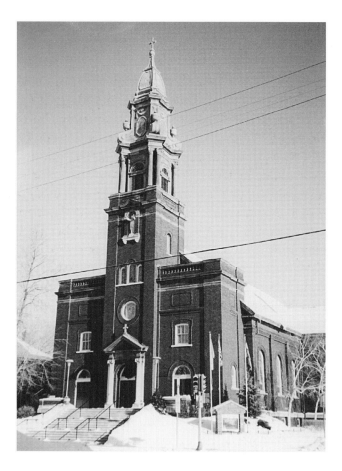

## ST. CYRIL'S

*Slovak wording appears on the exquisite stained glass windows of St. Cyril's. The Slovak crest is emblazoned above the stage in the school with the motto "Za Boha a Narod," which means "For God and country." A linden tree from the homeland shades the front of the building. An annual Slovak Mass is celebrated on February 14, the Feast Day of Saints Cyril and Methodius.*

In 1875, the Central European Slovak people began to arrive from their homeland west of the Ukraine. The origins of the Slovak culture date back eleven centuries when the Greek apostles Sts. Cyril and Methodius introduced Christianity along with the Glagolitic alphabet.

The Slovak people maintained their culture through centuries of domination. Ruled by the Hungarian Magyars after 900 A.D., then by the Austro-Hungarian Empire beginning in the 1800s, Slovaks experienced a steady repression of their customs and traditions. Denied civil rights and even forced to adopt Hungarian names, few Slovaks received more than a basic elementary education. So, priests became educational and cultural leaders as well as spiritual ones.

Repression, as well as harsh economic conditions in the last half of the nineteenth century, caused many Slovaks to leave their homeland for America. The immigrants moved first to the industrial northeastern United States. But as early as 1875, some Slovaks ventured west to Minnesota and found work in the mills and foundries near St. Anthony.

At first, the Slovaks settled near their European neighbors, the Czechs, in the area known as the "Bohemian Flats" located on the southeast banks of the Mississippi near the University of Minnesota campus. As the years passed, many of these immigrants moved to homes in Northeast. Some of the first Slovak pioneers included George and John Gogola, John Zelenak, Joseph Martonik, and Thomas Ovshak.

In 1888, a group of Slovak men organized Saints Cyril and Methodius Lodge, a benevolent organization to aid widows and orphans. The majority of the Slovaks were Catholic and, at first, worshiped at Holy Cross Church with the Poles. But, like most ethnic groups, the Slovaks wanted their own parish. Lodge members established a special fund for the construction of a church. Lodge representative John Brehovic visited other Slovak churches to raise funds for the building. Donations eventually totaled over $700.

John Langa and John Kertis found a site for the church at the corner of Sixteenth Avenue and Main Street Northeast. Church members purchased the property for $1,800 in 1888. Parishioners John Brehovic, Michael Hreha, George Kacmaryk, Andrew Majher, John Martonik, Andrew Olcha, and John Ovshak approached Bishop John Ireland for permission to begin construction.

The delegation proposed naming the new congregation for the apostles to the Slovaks, Saints Cyril and Methodius, but the bishop felt one name would be sufficient. So, the Church of St. Cyril incorporated in February 1891, and Bishop Ireland appointed a Slovakian Franciscan, Father John Ladislas Zavadan, as the first pastor.

Upon his arrival, Father Zavadan boarded with the priests of Holy Cross while making plans for his new parish. Builders finished the $6,000 structure by 1893 and a nearby home became the rectory. Father Francis Hrachovsky succeeded Zavadan in 1895 and built a new rectory in 1904. When officials of the Northern Pacific railroad proposed an elevated road along Main Street in 1909, they purchased the land the church and rectory occupied with the agreement both structures would be relocated. True to their promise, railroad officials arranged the move to Thirteenth Avenue and Third Street Northeast.

Parishioners began planning for a new St. Cyril in 1914, and workers completed the $85,000 edifice by 1917. In 1937, the School Sisters of Notre Dame came from Mankato to teach at a new parish school.

*St. Mary's Lodge, branch No.3 of the First Catholic Labor's Union 1930s.*

## ST. MARY'S
## ORTHODOX CATHEDRAL

*The icon of the Protection of the Most Holy Theotokos is displayed on the arch above the altar in St. Mary's Orthodox Cathedral. Purchased from Lvov, Russia in 1892, this symbol commemorates the Blessed Virgin Mary's appearance at Constantinople. In this rendering, John the Baptist and Moses support her and several saints accompany her.*

Eastern Europeans began to arrive in large numbers in Minneapolis by the 1870s. These immigrants represented several diverse cultures with complex backgrounds. More than formal political boundaries, the allegiance of these people depended on the regions of their birth. And although the people spoke similar languages, often collectively referred to as Slavish, distinct dialects segregated the groups from each other. Among these European groups were Carpatho-Rusins, Ukrainians, Ruthenians, and Russians.

Like other European nationalities, these immigrants left their homelands as a result of overpopulation and changes in the economy. After the Austro-Hungarian Empire divided, conditions worsened as rural landowners and workers became unemployed, landless laborers. Led by George Homzik, the first East Slavs arrived in Minnesota in 1877. Men found work in the railroad yards, in sawmills, and in flour mills.

While most East Slavs practiced the Catholic religion, they belonged to the Byzantine Rite Catholic Church or the Eastern Orthodox Catholic Church. The Slavish immigrants attending German or Polish Catholic churches missed the Byzantine ritual and Slavonic language of their homeland churches and feared the loss of their unique traditions. The Minneapolis Rusins brought Eastern Rite priests to baptize and offer liturgy, but visits by these clergy were infrequent.

Father John Voliansky, a Galician priest from Pennsylvania, urged the immigrants to establish their own Byzantine church. And in 1886, a committee led by Peter Kuchechka purchased property for a church at Seventeenth Avenue and Fifth Street Northeast. The men of the parish, led by carpenters Peter Dzubay, Jr., and Stephen Reshetar, built the wooden structure of St. Mary's Greek and Catholic Church, which was dedicated in 1889. The members requested a priest for their newly formed church from a bishop in Hungary, and the bishop accommodated by sending Father Alexis Toth to serve as pastor.

Like many Byzantine priests, Father Toth had been married. And when he sought diocesan authorization to serve the parish, Archbishop John Ireland denied Father Toth permission. Ireland also refused to acknowledge the legitimacy of the Byzantine Church in his diocese and ordered St. Mary's Catholics to attend the Polish Roman Catholic Church. At this point, the Slavs parted company with the Roman Catholic Diocese of St. Paul, and Bishop Vladimir Sokolovsky welcomed the parish members into the Russian Orthodox Diocese.

In 1897, parishioners opened a school which offered classes in both English and Russian. Fire destroyed the first St. Mary's Church in 1904, and members built a larger church. The first Orthodox seminary in the United States opened in 1905 in Minneapolis. Young men interested in the Byzantine priesthood no longer needed to travel to Russia for schooling.

*First Russian church parish school in the United States 1892.*

## ST. JOHN THE BAPTIST
## AND ST. CONSTANTINE

*St. Constantine's Church features an exotic Oriental blue, gold, and red dome supported by four arches. Inside the building on the ceiling of the main dome is the painted image of Christ within an eight-pointed star. Christ appears as the Apocalyptic Pantocrator with his right hand lifted in a blessing. Around the base of the dome, written in Ukrainian, is the inscription, "Thou shalt love the Lord thy God with thy whole heart, and with thy whole soul, and with thy whole mind, and thy neighbors as thyself."*

Religious politics spurred a second local church for the Slavs. In Europe, Hungarian leaders, fearful of the spread of the Russian Orthodox Church in America, lobbied the Vatican to establish Byzantine Rite Catholicism for the Slav immigrants. A papal representative visited Minneapolis and found Carpathian families would welcome a Byzantine Rite parish. This time, Bishop Ireland gave his blessing, providing the priests practiced celibacy. In 1907, Michael Rushin, Vasil Kanya, Stephen Hudak, Nick Dano, and Nick Serbanic purchased the old Polish church and moved the building to the corner of Twenty-second Avenue and Third Street Northeast, a few blocks from St. Mary's Orthodox Cathedral. Father J. A. Zaklynsky offered the first Greek Catholic Mass sanctioned by the Roman Catholic diocese on Thanksgiving Day in 1907.

By 1910, a community of 350 East Slav families lived along Fifth Street from Tenth to Eighteenth Avenues with the two churches the center of their religious and social lives. In 1926, parishioners constructed a new St. John the Baptist for the rapidly growing population and appointed Father J. P. Bihary to serve as pastor.

Intellectuals active in the Ukrainian independence movement comprised the group of East Europeans arriving from 1910 to 1917. This group, though small in number, displayed a strong national consciousness and promoted Ukrainian ethnicity and culture. Not entirely comfortable with the established Slav churches, the Ukrainians led by Michael Husak, Nicholas Mandzen, and Timothy Wozniak, organized St. Constantine Byzantine Rite Church in 1912. For the original seventy-two families of the parish, a hall at Twenty-second Avenue and Fifth Street Northeast functioned as a temporary worship center. The next year, parishioners purchased property at Sixth Street and University Avenue and began building an $8,000 church.

St. Constantine had a difficult beginning. Each of the first priests stayed only a few months, and strained financial obligations marred the new community's cohesiveness. Then with the outbreak of World War I in 1914, immigration virtually halted. But the years following the war brought both a revitalization of the Ukrainian national consciousness and renewed

the tensions between church members. Subsequently, a group left St. Constantine and joined the new Ukrainian Autocephalous Orthodox Church.

In 1925, St. Constantine's members purchased a building at Jackson and Summer Streets for the Ukrainian Educational Home, a center for cultural and social activities. Folk dancing groups, a drama society, and an orchestra used this building for meetings and events. Years later, the structure was moved to 301 Main Street Northeast and renamed Ukrainian Culture Center.

*Ukrainian dance ensemble.*

## ST. MARON'S

*As the only Catholic denomination from the Middle East, the Maronite church employs a unique symbolism, and St. Maron's contains examples of this rich legacy. Six stained glass windows called Rabboula characterize many of this community's most meaningful symbols. Peacocks represent everlasting life, an arch portrays support, and three stars on the Blessed Virgin Mary illustrate her roles as daughter, spouse, and mother.*

The first middle-Eastern immigrants to Minnesota were the Syrians. They began to arrive in Northeast Minneapolis in the 1880s from Bijdarfel, Batroun, Jdabra, and other villages south of Tripoli and settled near Marshall and Main Streets. A large portion of the immigrants came from small villages in the Mount Lebanon district, a coastal mountain region between the port cities of Beirut and Tripoli. After this area gained independence as the country of Lebanon in 1946, a renewed national consciousness spurred immigrants from that part of the country to think of themselves as Lebanese instead of Syrian.

By 1895, thirty Lebanese families lived in Northeast Minneapolis and, in that year's census, all listed their addresses as Mike Henne's store at 123 Main Street. As a wholesaler of rosaries, jewelry, and notions, Mike Henne helped many of the male immigrants start businesses as peddlers. The women often supplemented this income by taking in sewing and laundry. Many immigrants saved the profits from peddling and opened small shops which remained family-owned for generations. By 1938, Lebanese families owned four dry goods stores and five groceries in Northeast Minneapolis.

Although many Lebanese Americanized their names upon arrival in the United States, they maintained their religious allegiance to the Lebanese Orthodox Church or the Maronite Catholic Church. St. Maron's Church parishioners first met under the leadership of Reverend A. Eito in a private residence at 321 Main Street Northeast in 1906.

Eventually, over 100 members joined this newly emerging parish. Reverend E. El-Kouri purchased the Church of Our Lady of Mount Carmel at 625 Main Street Northeast for the growing community in 1919. The parish population increased to 450 members by 1948, so members built a larger church at 219 Sixth Avenue Northeast. The new church, built with the guidance of Reverend Assemani, was considered a shrine in honor of Maronite saints.

\* \* \*

Along with the new immigrants, came their need to firmly establish new traditions and lifestyles to replace those left behind. In some cases, the freedom to construct a new culture came as a welcome opportunity to relieve the immigrants from their hardships. But these new residents also realized the need to preserve the best qualities of their homeland. From the haste with which the groups organized churches upon their arrival, the immigrants clearly associated their country's finer characteristics with a religion. In this new land, religion served to affirm their ancestral heritage as well as establish a new legacy for their children. And no place is this cultural phenomena more apparent than in Northeast Minneapolis—a neighborhood that has a church on almost every corner.

*Note. 13th and Monroe St. NE is listed in the Guinness Book of World Records as the only place on earth with 4 churches on one block.

*Holy Cross Band.*

*Street Scene along Central Avenue showing Mrs. Johnson's Store. Schooner's Bar and Gustafson's Jewelers in the background 1944.*

# 4 A Sense of Place

## *Grain Belt Brewery Tour Illuminates Northeast Building's Colorful History.*

**By Amy I. Clements**
*Northeaster*: September 24, 1986

When Stanley Mrugala first started work at the Grain Belt Brewery's bottling plant in the 1930s, they bottled beer by hand with some help from conveyer belts.

Bottles filled with beer pumped over from the brew house traveled on the belt to the pasteurizer and labeler and the waiting crew for casing. For many years two men, one on each side of a table, put the bottles in cases.

By 1974, when Mrugala left, all the casing was done at the touch of a button, he said, and fewer workers were needed to operate the bottling plant.

His uncle also worked at the brewery, from about 1899 until the brewery at Broadway and Marshall Streets NE closed for a few years during prohibition in the 1920s. He was there when horses left the brewery's iron gates for beer deliveries. The beer was later shipped by rail and then by truck.

Mrugala, 74, has fond memories of his days at the brewery. He remembers the brewery floors being so clean one "could eat off them." The view of the machinery in the brewhouse was overwhelming, he said, and "the brass just shined."

He also remembers the tourists enjoying beer and pretzels in the brewery park at the end of the tour, and couples having their wedding pictures taken in the same park. Area residents would also go to the brewery to get the good-tasting water from the artesian well.

He made many friends there too, he said. A group of the workers played softball on a grassy area near the brewery, and they organized bowling teams.

John Szymanski used to be "number one man" in the Grain Belt brewhouse (a separate building from the bottling plant). He was in charge of filling the 510-barrel brew kettles and boiling the liquid that would become beer.

As it entered the 1970s, he said, the Grain Belt Brewery was one of the largest and cleanest regional breweries in the country. The brewery produced one million barrels of beer a year at its peak.

The brewhouse was immaculate, with spotless, tiled floors and shining, stainless steel and copper kettles, he said.

It was also bustling with employees around the clock,

*Minneapolis Brewing Company (Grain Belt) 1922.*

all wearing fresh white uniforms and boots, and during the day a round of tourists went through the building every half hour or so.

A present day tour of the Brewery, built in 1891, is desolate by comparison, as the building has been empty for 10 years and has an uncertain future.

The effect of 10 years of vacancy is more evident inside the brewhouse than outside. A group of city officials, Minneapolis Heritage Preservation Commission members, representatives of building owner Irwin Jacobs, and residents toured the brewhouse recently and saw the ravages of 10 years as well as the evidence of a once-beautiful interior.

Outside, one is impressed by the stately, German castle-like appearance of the large limestone and brick structure.

Then, one notices the towers on the uneven roof line; two steep, pointed towers, a shorter, square tower, and a dome-shaped tower topped by a weather vane.

Next, the eye settles on the words "Grain Belt," conspicuously displayed in the center of the long roof line, before moving down to the signs of age and vacancy-broken windows, large boarded windows and a "Private Property—Keep Out" sign in a stone archway.

Inside, the tourists walked across floors covered with pigeon droppings, climbed stairs that had steps completely or partially missing, and saw huge, stainless steel vats that used to hold beer and a battered control panel that will never be used again. Very few pieces of the equipment associated with beer making were left because most were sold in a 1976 auction.

Dark, enclosed rooms where no sunlight reached and wide open areas drenched with sunlight provide sharp contrasts. Ornate metal stairways, light green in color, wind their way to some of the uneven floor levels in the building, while wooden stairs against one wall lead to others. Two boilers that heat all of the buildings on the site occupy an adjacent boiler house.

After a long climb to the top of the building and a short climb up a ladder, the tourists stood on a roof with a close-up view of the Grain Belt weather vane and a dazzling view of Minneapolis.

When the Grain Belt Brewery was formed in 1890, it was called the Minneapolis Brewing and Malting Company. It kept that name until 1967. The brewery was created by the merger of four smaller breweries; the John Orth Brewing Company, the Heinrich Brewing Association, the Germania Brewing Company and the F. D. Norenberg Brewery and Malt House.

The Orth Brewing Company owned the land that later contained the Grain Belt brewhouse. Founder John Orth, born in Alsace, was the first brewer and German-born settler to arrive in St. Anthony, the settlement that became part of Minneapolis.

The Victorian brewhouse, designed by the architectural and engineering firm Wolff and Lehle of Chicago, is a conglomerate of many styles. The building's four-part facade, five to six stories high, is said to represent the four breweries that formed the Minneapolis Brewing company, and the four main brewing processes that were carried on within the brewhouse walls.

The building is in effect five interconnected buildings with different numbers and levels of floors in each section, said a Minneapolis Community Development Agency report. The number of floors range from two to six, and ceiling heights range from 7 to over 60 feet. The building layout was effective for the multi-process brewing operation.

The current owner, Irwin Jacobs, purchased the brewery site in 1975 and closed the brewery when he sold the Grain Belt label to the G. Heileman Brewing Company in 1976. Jacobs applied for a permit to demolish the building in 1977, but after a swell of opposition from residents and government officials, the Heritage Preservation Commission (HPC) and the City Council designated it a historic landmark. That designation requires Jacobs to obtain HPC and city approval to demolish the building.

Developers have found redevelopment of the brewhouse economically unfeasible, and Jacobs representatives say maintaining the building is costly. Jacobs again recently requested permission to demolish the building, and the HPC denied the request. He has also offered to donate the brewhouse to the city, but city officials have not decided whether to accept the offer.

Everyone with an interest in the brewhouse is waiting to see whether a Minneapolis firm's forthcoming proposal to develop the site is workable.

*Alfred Erlandson loading bran from Grain Belt Brewery to take to dairy farm near Lake Nokomis where he worked about 1908.*

*Little Sisters of the Poor, St. Joseph's Home for the Aged, now Stonehouse Square Apartments 1978–79.*

# Little Sisters of the Poor
## What Goes on Here..

**By Brenda Ueland**

*Minneapolis Times*: January 21, 1944

In France about 1792 there was a humble, industrious girl, Jeanne Jugan. She and her two friends, a grocer's daughter and a sailor's daughter, liked to "practice hospitality" to the poor. After awhile they wrote out their rule of life: to take care of destitute old people and to trust in God for whatever food, clothing, was needed.

This was the beginning of the Little Sisters of the Poor. The first Little Sisters came to Minneapolis in 1895 and built their huge yellow brick structure, melancholy and picturesque. It lies athwart Second St. N.E. A few blocks away there is the dirty grey Mississippi among railroad yards, and warehouses.

Now there are 14 sisters and Sister Pascaline is the Mother Superior. Alone, without a single servant of any kind, they take care of 130 old people in this large four-story building. I have been there three times but I have seen only one Little Sister, because they must all work so hard. In midwinter the old people fall sick. And they die too.

And this one Little Sister thought it was better for me not to know her name. "It is enough to speak of Mother Pascaline," she said. She has a waxen, pale face, full of joyfulness, and grey eyes behind aseptically shining spectacles, and she wears a starched white bonnet tied sprucely under her chin. She is continuously smiling, and

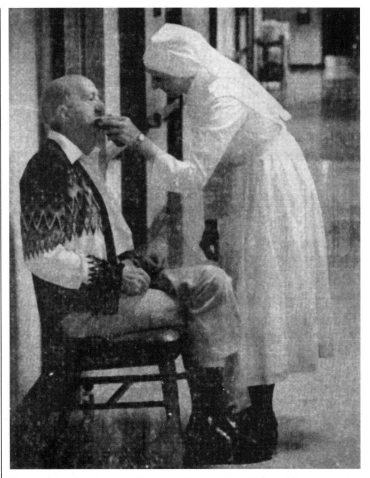

*Sister Maria gives a shave to Lawrence Schneider, a resident at home in fourth floor hallway of the Holy Family residence 1982.*

naive and pure in heart, and all the time she has a kind of invisible fun in her.

First she showed me the chapel. "We are very proud of our chapel." It is two stories high, like a pretty little church, and it is like the warm hearth of this whole building. They just love their chapel. There is a statue of St. Michael the archangel and the fatherly St. Joseph. Father Turgeon had told me that St. Joseph is their special saint and helper. They will put a potato in his hand if they need potatoes, say. . . .

"It is true?" I asked her.

"It really is," she said, so pleased to tell about it. There were a few old ladies in there, and an old man with thick hair. " They come and stay all afternoon. You see we believe that Jesus is right in here. He is right in here all the time. So they like come and talk to Him, all afternoon, and they enjoy it."

In the women's sitting room they were sewing, dreaming vacantly. They talk little I think, and even curiosity seems to be almost nonexistent. There was an unbelievably bent old woman in the dining room scraping half an apple with a knife, "She is the very oldest—she is 96," and the Little Sister spoke to her uncomprehending face in a casual, mild way.

"It is their afternoon out," she said, "and here are their hats"—paper boxes piled on the table. She lifted a lid to show me a little old-lady hat with its thin flowers and finery.

I wrung it out of her that the old men make their beds, keep their dormitory shipshape, "even a little better than the women, I am afraid." In their smoking room, four of them were playing cards. And in that silence of withdrawn, silent, aged people, one man slammed a card down and cried "Ha," and laughed. The little Sister liked that noise and gaiety. And so did I.

"When did you become a Little Sister?"

"Forty years ago."

"And why did you?"

She laughs at such a question and said with smiling earnestness "Because I loved God and wanted to help Him. And I loved the poor."

"Well, why do you love the poor? I know why you SHOULD—and why you have sympathy for them. But what is YOUR reason."

"Well Our Lord loved the poor and wanted to be with them and always chose that. And so we just try to be like Him. That is all it is."

The 14 Little Sisters have their daily works all arranged. Two of them go out on a truck to collect food, coal, groceries. Many big shops and stores give these things at regular intervals. Some of the Little Sisters go about asking people for money, rich and poor, and St. Joseph of course leads them to where it will be gladly given.

When I said goodbye, at the entrance, on a little stand there is a small statue of the fatherly saint. We spoke of the tiny American flag some one had put there (because he would like it) and someone had put a plant there for him too. And I noticed just then a slot. You see St. Joseph had invisibly pulled my sleeve and told me to give something. And so I did.

*Margaret Barry House 759 Pierce Street Northeast 1925.*

# *Heart Centers of Minneapolis.*

*Minneapolis Tribune:* March 9, 1924

### *Margaret Barry Settlement House, Community Fund Institution, Serves Needs of Neighborhood in Athletics, Health Clinics, Home Courses*

With a total aggregate attendance in all departments of 9,684 in the past year Margaret Barry settlement house, a Community Fund institution, located at the corner of Broadway and Pierce Street Northeast, is serving the needs of its community as a neighborhood center.

Ask anyone in the neighborhood a question and the reply invariably is "You can find out about it at Margaret Barry House." There is scarcely a home in the district lying between the gas house and the gravel pits that is not represented in one or more of the activities at the neighborhood house from athletics to health clinics, from sewing classes to Boy Scouting, from craft work to methods of housekeeping.

Foreign born groups within a radius of two miles of the settlement are among its loyal supporters. Among these special groups are Italians, Russians, Poles, French, Lithuanians and Ukrainians.

"Americanization is one of the largest tasks," said Miss Marion Schaller, who has just become the new head worker, "Americanization does not mean instructing the foreign born in such matters as who is president of the United States, and who is the mayor of the city. It consists

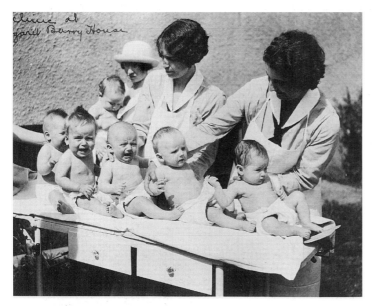

*Baby Clinic showing mothers how to give a bath at Margaret Barry House in 1925.*

in helping the foreign born to adapt their entire mode of living to American conditions.

It often means rebuilding friendly relationships between parents and their children in cases where the latter have outgrown the former. Outgrown is the very word to describe it. The children become familiar with English. They absorb American institutions readily through the schools. They are Americanized before they are 10 years old and quite naturally they begin to feel that father and mother are years and years behind the times. Consequently they are likely to disregard all advice of their parents, being unable to distinguish what is good and what is not in accord with the present standards of living."

Miss Schaller believes that American ideas of conduct can be taught in no surer way then through athletics. There are eight basketball teams at the settlement. There will be two baseball teams, a diamond ball team and many intramural teams this year. Margaret Barry house is also the center of neighborhood health activities having infant welfare, dental and general health clinics to which those in the community who are unable to afford services of a physician are admitted. Health lessons taught at the settlement carry such weight with those aided that the general principles emphasized are readily accepted even when they clash with old-country ideas and customs.

*Lantern slide photo of child care service at Northeast Neighborhood House 1919.*

*Boys in football helmets talking to Mr. Gilman on the steps of Northeast Neighborhood House in 1927.*

## *Northeast Neighborhood House*

1929 Second St. NE. The problems facing the early immigrants were high infant mortality, disease, delinquency and crime, poverty and ignorance. The Northeast Neighborhood House was started in response to these problems. The people came for nutrition classes, community dramas or sometimes just to take a shower. The roots go back to the 1880s when Ply-mouth Congregational Church established the Emmanuel Sunday School Mission at Drummond Hall at 1429 Second Street. The Protestant Mission found it difficult to attract members because of the influx of Eastern Europeans who were predominantly Catholic, and they closed in 1912. In 1915, Mrs. Charles C. Bovey reorganized Drummond Hall as a settlement house. After a complete remodeling, NENH reopened on January 20, 1915 offering classes in sewing, cooking, carpentry, dancing and athletics. 246 children signed up on the very first day. The first head worker, Robbins Gilman had recently arrived from New York and asked the children what kind of activities they would be interested in. He then hired a youth worker and proceeded to develop these activities. Gilman also started an employment bureau to protect immigrant workers and to expose sweatshop conditions. Training programs were set up for women seeking jobs in domestic work and care of electrical equipment. A day nursery was set up for working women. Miss Woods School for Kindergarten teachers opened a demonstration kindergarten at NENH. A dental clinic opened in 1918 and was the first of its kind in Minneapolis. The gym wing was added in 1927. English classes and lectures were given to help the immigrants become naturalized citizens. All the ethnic groups got together for the first time in 1918 to celebrate their customs and traditions. They called it Neighbor Day, which was celebrated on Flag Day. The Neighborhood House was also headquarters for the sale of thrift stamps or ration cards. The set up of the Red Cross, the Girls' Liberty League, and the draft registration brought many people who had never been in before. The families of Northeast Minneapolis responded whole heartedly to the liberty bond drive. Sales from the first ward exceeded $450,000. Solicitors found that the Polish people rarely refused to buy a bond. The same generosity was demonstrated during the Red Cross drive of 1917. The Catholic priests urged the people to express their patriotism through these drives. During the social reform movement, the people of the community were concerned about delinquency and youth gangs. Early activities for young people at the settlement house included a pool room and the athletic teams were given support through the North East Boosters formed in 1954. The Goldbricks, a northeast community service group, began as a youth club in 1949. Day camps for children were offered. One of the most familiar to northeast children was summer resident camp at Camp Bovey, in northern Wisconsin, which was acquired in 1950. In 1948, Lester Schaeffer succeeded Gilman as director and in 1973, Joseph Holewa took over as executive director. Holewa is the only one who grew up in the neighborhood. In 1963, NENH merged with the Margaret Barry House, and became East Side Neighborhood Services.

*Edison High School 700-22nd Ave. NE 1950s.*

## *Early Edison*
## *Vaudeville, Popcorn, Sunlight Dances, Sodas at Schrags.*

**By Tim Fuehrer**
*Northeaster*: May 17, 1989

Herbert Hoover was in the White House and a new Chevy coupe cost $669, but no one could afford one.

"It was a pity too," said Steve Subak, "Gas only cost 11 cents a gallon. But it was a good life when I graduated from Edison in 1929. But we had our friends and got together often."

Subak, the chairman for the Edison High School class of 1929 reunion committee, and friends still get together often. The reunion group, which includes the January and June 1929 and January 1930 classes, meets annually.

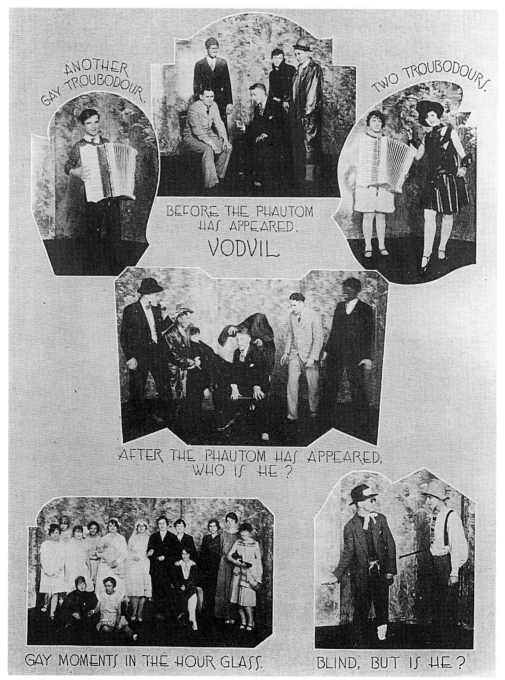

ANOTHER GAY TROUBODOUR.

TWO TROUBODOURS.

BEFORE THE PHAUTOM HAS APPEARED.

VODVIL

AFTER THE PHAUTOM HAS APPEARED,
WHO IS HE ?

GAY MOMENTS IN THE HOUR GLASS.

BLIND, BUT IS HE ?

*Vaudeville skits put on by Edison students 1930.*

Reunions were held every five years, Subak said, "but in 1979, we started meeting every year. It's a great opportunity to meet with old friends."

Ann (Horney) McLaughlin, who also serves on the reunion committee, and classmate Emma (Larson) Wines agree. "It's something to look forward to each year," they said.

Last year, 103 attended the reunion, Subak said. At least 100 are expected at the reunion this year, scheduled Sept. 14 at the Nicollet Island Inn.

Edison High School first opened Sept. 5, 1922, under the name Northeast High School. The new school, built at a cost of more than $800,000 had 1,650 students in grades 7–11.

Subak first attended Edison as a seventh grader in 1923. "The school was so big. It was organized confusion," he said. Among his many activities, Subak became active in the school's Hi-Y Club, which was affiliated with the YMCA.

One of the club's first meetings turned out to be Subak's first experience with chow mein. "I wasn't used to it, " he said, "and didn't like it. I dumped it all out. But I stayed with Hi-Y. Religiously and socially it was an excellent character builder."

Wilson's Confectionery at 22nd and Monroe was a popular student hangout. "We weren't supposed to go there during the school day, but we'd sneak over," Wines said.

Near the store, a horse drawn popcorn wagon was kept in an open field. The field later became Pete Guzy Field.

"We'd go over there and get popcorn all of the time," McLaughlin said. "The principal, Mr. Louis Cook, didn't approve. He called special assemblies and asked us 'Does he feed you with one hand while he's feeding the horse with the other?'"

*A heavy date 1935.*

Vaudeville acts, performed regularly in the school auditorium, were popular, Subak said. "Peter Kranak and Alex Boris had an act that kept us in stitches," he said.

According to Wines, McLaughlin was also a popular vaudeville musical performer. "She still is very active," Wines said, "and performs in a group with her daughter and granddaughter."

McLaughlin said music teacher Elmer Sodergren made

*Edison Senior Prom of January 1935. Proms were divided into two sessions of which the parents and faculty were invited to attend.*

you like music. "To this day, it's something I've kept up with and still enjoy. And every year, Miss (Ruth) Tupper ran the class play. It was always Shakespeare."

Other regular school events were "Sunlight" dances in the gymnasium. "They had them about once a month in the afternoon," Subak said. "The school band played. That's where most of us learned how to dance."

On prom night, the gymnasium was decorated so much "you didn't know you were in a gym," Subak said. "Girls wore their best dresses and us boys our best suit and a tie. And we walked and we had to be home by 11 P.M."

Wines said, "Everyone walked. There were few cars and we never expected a ride."

McLaughlin added, "Girls never had corsages and at the prom all we had was punch and cookies."

Skating at Jackson Square was popular. "For most of us that was what we did during the winter," Wines said, "that and sodas and sundaes at Schrags at 20th and Central."

Wines remembers getting back her locker deposit. "It was only 50 cents, but we thought we were millionaires," she said. "We ran over to Schrags and blew it all on sundaes."

Another classmate, Joseph Manchak, "was an excellent singer and formed his own dance band," Subak said, "and played at our reunions for several years."

"We were right in the middle of the Depression and didn't have much money," Wines said. "But we sure had a great time."

Subak described his graduation ceremony as "very dignified."

"We got dressed up in our suits and ties," he said. "We didn't wear robes. The school orchestra played 'The War March of the Priests' and Manchak sang 'On the Road to Mandalay.' I remember the feeling of release I got when Mr. Cook gave me my diploma."

After commencement, Subak and some of his friends "drove out to a lake and sat around and talked about our futures. I got a shirt and tie for a graduation present, not a new car."

At the 57th reunion, Subak said, "When we were in high school, pizza, frozen orange juice, instant coffee and McDonalds were unheard of. Fast food was something you ate during Lent.

"Grass was something you mowed, coke was something you drank and pot something you cooked in. 'Made in Japan' meant junk and at 5- and 10-cent stores, you could buy something for 5 and 10 cents."

"But there are some things that never change—our ability to have a good time, and our pride in and love for our classmates and our Alma Mater."

*Lowry Elementary School 1920.*

# 63-Year-Old Lowry School Closed:
# Reminiscences of a School That Won't Open this Fall..

**By Imogene Erie Schopf**
*Minneapolis Argus:* August 16,1978

### THOMAS LOWRY SCHOOL
### Born — 1915        Died — 1978

"Mourned by students and teachers, past and present. We are grateful for the many hours we have spent in your hallowed halls. They will remove you from our presence but they can never remove you from our hearts."

Sentimental? Corny? Maybe. But how can you write objectively about the school that sheltered you and protected you from harm that warm, September day, your first full day away from home?

It's official now, Lowry School is really closing. I had known it for some time but, somehow, reading about it in the paper had a strange impact upon me.

Living only a block away these many years I had grown used to seeing its red brick walls looming in between the large, shady elms that formed a majestic, green arch on Lincoln St. I thought of all the sunsets that I had watched disappear behind its massive walls and wondered if I could watch the cold steel wrecking ball that would one day soon send it's crushing blows to the school where I had spent so much of my life. I, who became sentimental over every old car we had to part with.

I remembered how the bright lights from every room would illuminate the whole block those dark nights, in the fall of the year, when open house was held. And how the floors and desks smelled of fresh polish as the school put its best foot forward to receive the parents who came to view their children's work.

I thought about the kindergarten and the playhouse that we were allowed to play in when we had been especially well-behaved, and remembered how proud I was of the oil cloth doll I had made, all by myself. Well, almost. Years later I was to find myself leaving my son in the same room and feeling bad because, unconcerned, he merely said, "Bye, Mom," as I turned my back to leave him on his first day of school.

As a small child I remember coming home from late outings with my parents and sleepily opening my eyes to see Lowry School towering before us as we drove up 29th Ave. I knew we were almost home.

It was more than a school. It had become a landmark and a source of pride for the people who lived "on the hill." The community had become as much a part of it as it had become a part of the community.

During the war years we waited in lines there to receive our ration books and to hear all the latest news about the neighborhood boys who were away fighting the war. Sometimes it was to offer sympathy to the relatives of those who were wounded and, sometimes, those who would never come back. We patriotically flattened all of our tin cans and, along with any other scrap metal we could find, brought them to school for the scrap iron drives for "Our" school.

*Paper Drive of Prescott School in 1924. Elementary schools held paper sales to raise money for their school. A prize was given to the room that collected the most newspapers.*

There were the paper sales when we kids would try our best to help our room win the prize for bringing the most papers and magazines. Sometimes we'd sneak away with a comic book or two. Time flew, and it didn't seem that many years later when we found ourselves adults, back on the same school parking lot, helping our own kids to win the "big" prize.

It was the place we stood in line to vote on election day and engaged in friendly teasing with our neighbors if their choice of candidate wasn't ours.

There were the PTA meetings, the Fall Carnivals, the Spring Picnics and the hundred other ways in which the school became a part of our lives. Now it was to be over.

Much as a stepparent can replace a natural parent, a new school can replace an old school, but it's never quite the same, is it? The ties that bind will always be there. You were ours.

# The East-Side Fire:
# The Tragic Day, August 13, 1893,
# When Part of Minneapolis Was Devastated by Fire

**By Joseph W. Zalusky**
*Hennepin County History:* Spring,1960

There are still many old timers among us who remember when Minneapolis—then a city of 185,700 people—was visited by a terrible conflagration: the most widespread in its history and one entailing a money loss of over one million dollars (and that was a lot of money in the year 1893).

There were two centers of fire, one among the factories on Nicollet Island below Central Avenue (now East Hennepin), and the other in the lumber milling district in Northeast Minneapolis.

The fire began on lower Nicollet Island and it is generally conceded that it jumped to the mill district through the medium of flying sparks (a distance of about one-half mile), to the dry piles of lumber, shingles and laths which were stored on what is still known as Boom Island. Once the flames leaped to the mass of dry timber, it was soon out of control. The heat became so great that soon the flames leaped across the narrow channel to the mainland where nearly everything in its path was consumed.

The extent of the fire was the area bounded by the Mississippi River on the West, 6th Avenue N.E., on the South to about 15th Avenue N.E., on the North, and Marshall Street on the East. In some places the fire reached Main Street N.E., where the fireman made a final determined stand.

According to the 1893 file in our library, the area consisted of about 30 blocks, each 330 feet square, streets not included. The map shows that in this area there were: 160 houses, 58 accessory buildings, two ice-houses, one shingle mill, one planing mill, sash and door factory, one warehouse, the Minneapolis Brewing Company buildings, one soap factory, two office buildings and millions of board feet of lumber; much of this was destroyed.

On Nicollet Island two ice-houses, one boiler works, one box factory and a carriage went up in smoke. It was the assessors belief that 200 families were made homeless involving nearly 1,000 people. Many Polish people with large families and unable to speak English, were burned out. There were many rumors of people killed, but nearly all were rumors and appeared to be without foundation. Many children became lost from their families but after the excitement subsided they were found and reunited. The St. Anthony Turner Hall, a two-story frame building, was offered for the use of hundreds of the homeless for the night.

All the way from Sixth Avenue N.E. to 16th Avenue at Marshall Street there were extraordinary scenes of great excitement. Families whose homes were endangered by the spreading flames were loading household goods and carting them away to places of safety in wagons and vehicles of all description. Those who could afford it, hired expressmen and it was estimated that fully 100 expressmen were engaged in moving goods from houses. The poorer people carried their household effects in their arms, but most of them seemed to be content in saving their lives and what material they could.

Aside from the property loss which was disastrous to several of the most enterprising of the lumbermen and manufacturers of Minneapolis, the catastrophe bore heavily on labor. Many men were thrown out of work and the suffering was considerable in view of the fact that the labor market was already heavily overstocked because of the dull times which had prevailed for several months.

Your editor saw the smoke from this fire and ran all the way to Nicollet Island where, after viewing the fire, crossed over the East Channel of the Mississippi River by the way of logs to get a clearer view (all the kids skipped logs in the' 90s). The fire was so hot here that the rails on the railroad right-of-way were twisted into all kinds of shapes by the heat. Because of the saw-dust [sic] and lumber the fire smoldered for more than two weeks. Forepaugh's Circus came into town over the Milwaukee Road on this day and pitched their tents on the circus grounds on 13th and Nicollet. After dinner the manager took a trip on horseback to find a bathing place for his herd of 12 elephants. Since elephants are fond of water they are given a bath whenever a deep place with a good approach and solid footing can be found. Otherwise, they are given a bath by means of a rubber hose. A large number of employees of the Forepaugh's Circus were interested in the East Side fire and said that the blaze was gotten up for their special entertainment.

# Connections – the Places We Remember

## AARON CARLSON MILLWORK

1505 Central Avenue NE, was started in 1891 by Aaron Carlson, a new arrival from Varmland, Sweden. In the early days of St. Anthony, Carlson designed and built a boat for Captain John Martin, a prominent figure in Minnesota history and grandfather of Earle Brown of the noted Earle Brown Farm. One of the millwork's first major projects was the American Swedish Institute. Other clients included the Ordway Music Theater in St. Paul, the Hilton Convention Center Hotel in Minneapolis, and both the Anoka and Ramsey County Courthouses. Today, the millwork company still occupies the original building and the owner, Paul Carlson, is the third generation of his family to oversee operations.

## ARION THEATER

2316 Central Avenue NE. In 1914 Jack Liebenberg and Seeman Kaplan built their first theater in Northeast Minneapolis. It was owned by Abraham A. Kaplan and managed by Louis Rubenstein. The building had a classical style, and the music was provided by an organ and Harry Maddy's Jazz orchestra, some of the finest musicians in that time period. Silent pictures cost ten cents for children and twenty cents for adults. The movie business boomed in 1914 because of the war in Europe. People wanted to see the update of the war. This was the introduction of the newsreel where information was given about other parts of the world, mostly Europe. One of the first films shown at the Arion was the Great Train Robbery. Filmed in 1903, it was packed with action, violence and frontier humor. In one scene, the director mounts the camera on top of a moving train. The last scene shows a shocking full screen closeup of a bandit firing his pistol at the audience. The Great Train Robbery introduced the Nickelodeons, functional, but not fancy movie theaters that swept across America in the 1910 era. The audience could get about an hour's worth of short films for a nickel.

## B. F. NELSON COMPANY

401 Main Street NE, began in 1865 when B. F. Nelson came to Minneapolis with $1 in his pocket and began rafting logs for $2 a day. Born in Kentucky to a family of modest means, Nelson interrupted his education to help support his ten siblings. As a result, he learned about logging on the Ohio River as a young boy of seventeen. After serving in the Confederacy, Nelson observed the ravages of the Civil War and decided to settle elsewhere. Descriptions of the fertile northlands led Nelson to Minnesota. Not long after his arrival, Nelson secured a government contract for $56 per day to provide the lumber necessary for preventing the collapse of St. Anthony Falls. His business grew, but when the lumber industry faltered, Nelson began manufacturing paper. He also discovered that by processing rags into pulp, saturating them with asphalt, and coating them with granules, he could produce a high-quality roofing material. After a century on the east bank of the Mississippi, the State Highway Department's plan for a new freeway forced the company to relocate to Chaska. The warehouse and carton plant are still located in Southeast Minneapolis.

*B.F. Nelson Company (formerly Dorman's Bank Bldg.) 402 NE Main Street 1895.*

## BLACKEY'S BAKERY

639 Twenty-second Avenue NE, has the only hearth oven left in the country. William Blackey and his wife Magdalene opened the bakery in 1919. During those first years, horse-drawn wagons delivered the products directly to the customer. The original hearth was enlarged and rebuilt in 1930. Families often brought turkeys, chickens, and hens to be roasted in the huge oven, which could accommodate over 400 chickens at a time. William and Magdalene's sons, Bud and George, managed the business for a time before selling the bakery. New owners Svea and Ingolf Ernst purchased Blackey's in 1990 and continue to use the old recipes and traditional baking methods. Workers still slide the bread into the oven on long paddles even though this extra attention may add to the cost. Loyalty among Blackey's bakers and drivers, many of whom have worked at the bakery for twenty years, remains strong.

## CREAM OF WHEAT

730 Stinson Boulevard, was born of desperation during the Panic of 1893 in Grand Forks, North Dakota. Tom Amidon, a flour miller by trade, approached his partners about selling the "breakfast porridge" his family loved in the commercial market. His partners agreed to ship some of the product, with their flour, to New York. Using scrap cardboard and old print plates to create colorful but inexpensive packaging, Amidon prepared the cereal for transport. Twelve hours after the shipment arrived in the East, the New York investors wired North Dakota to send more Cream of Wheat. As the popularity of the product increased, company owners decided to move to Minneapolis because of its proximity to wheat supplies and its advantageous shipping position. In 1962, Nabisco purchased the company.

## CROWN IRON WORKS

109–115 Second Avenue SE, opened in 1876 under the ownership of two Swedish immigrants. Both Andrew H. Nelson and E. Hernlund perceived a need for a blacksmith shop upon their arrival in the booming lumber town of St. Anthony. They began smithing on the river bank in a small wooden building adjacent to the falls and close to their lumber company clients. Herlund's son brought the mechanical engineering expertise to the firm, while Nelson was known as an artisan for his decorative wrought iron work. Later, the business moved to Northeast Minneapolis at Twelfth Avenue and Tyler Street. One of the company's most noteworthy projects was the Guarantee Loan Building, later renamed the Metropolitan Life Building, which was the first skyscraper west of the Mississippi. Although the business moved to Roseville, Crown Iron remains family-owned but with a drastically different product than the original rod iron and structural steel of yesteryear. Today, the business manufactures equipment used for the extraction and refining of cooking oil.

## DELMONICO'S ITALIAN FOODS

1112 Summer Street NE, stands across the street from Beltrami Park. Inside Louis Delmonico's Italian grocery, shelves line all walls and are jam packed with products. Employees use hooked poles to reach the highest shelves, while collapsible wooden boxes filled with orders stand on the counter waiting for delivery. The Delmonico brothers have owned and worked in the store since 1931. Delmonico still remembers when gypsies used to sweep through the neighborhood in horse-drawn carts. The brothers greet many customers by name and enjoy complimenting the ladies. Specialties include anise cookies and nine-inch donuts, fragrant Italian cheeses, marinated olives, and their own spaghetti sauce.

## ELSIE'S BOWLING CENTER

729 Marshall Street NE, is located in a building dating back to the early 1900s when the Sports Inn, owned by Grain Belt Brewery, and the Town Pump Bar were located in identical buildings across the street from each other. In 1956, Robert McGuffie purchased the Sports Inn, added on a restaurant decorated with a Scottish motif and named the new business Elsie's, after his daughter. Elsie Nelson requested that money raised from the restaurant's pull tabs be kept in the Northeast area and donated to Catholic Eldercare. Six more lanes were added on to the original ten in 1962. New owner, Robert Tuttle remodeled recently, and added on a banquet room. But the front of the building still contains the original bar that dates back to somewhere around the 1920s. Mike and Tim are now the managers, but Bill Nelson, Elsie's son, still comes in to help on a part time basis. The "lucky thirteen" tournaments held three times a year have been going strong since 1959. Like other Northeast businesses, some of the regulars have been coming in to bowl at Elsie's for over twenty-five years.

## EMILY'S LEBANESE DELICATESSEN

641 University Avenue NE, continues to offer ethnic food to Northeast's residents. Lebanese foods such as humus, stuffed grape leaves, and flat spinach pies tantalize returning patrons as well as newcomers to the establishment. The tabbouleh salad, made with parsley, tomatoes, and a spicy sauce called zlata is very popular. The owner Emily Awaijane was born in Batroun, Lebanon, and came to America in 1936. She spent almost forty years working in other restaurants before her family saved the money to open the delicatessen in an old duplex. Today, her kids run the shop.

# GLUEK'S BREWERY

Twenty-second and Marshall Street NE, was founded in 1857 during a tumultuous economy by Gottlieb Gluek, a German immigrant. In March of 1880, fire destroyed the wooden brewery building. Gluek began rebuilding immediately, and had nearly finished a new structure when he died. Construction continued, and Gluek's three sons completed two-story brick brewery. For a time, Gluek's was the oldest continuously operated business in Minneapolis. In the 1960s, however, business declined and the owners sold the company to competitor G. Heileman of LaCrosse, Wisconsin. Razing of the building occurred in 1966.

*Louis Gluek residence*
*2004 Marshall St. NE 1965.*

*Mississippi Brewery (later known as Gluek Brewery)*
*in 1872. Gottlieb Gluek is in center and Charles Gluek*
*is sitting on barrels on left.*

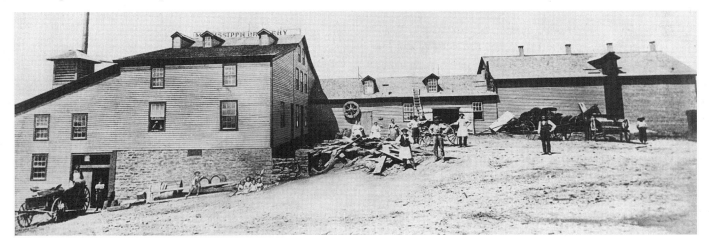

## GRAIN BELT BREWERY

1215 Marshall Street NE, formed upon the merger of four small brewers in 1893. During prohibition, the brewery was forced to close but opened the same day the amendment was repealed. Brewery fortunes continued to prosper throughout the postwar years, and supplied a strong economic presence to Northeast residents. Grain Belt Brewery provided thousands of jobs for the area's diverse ethnic groups over the years. Whether intentional or not, the architecture of the brewery imitated that of the old European breweries. Designated as a historical landmark in 1977, the building continues to receive its share of attention from visitors and residents alike.

## HOLLYWOOD THEATER

2815 Johnson St. NE. The Rubenstein family paid $100,000 to erect the Hollywood theater in 1935, and owned it until 1970. Charles Rubenstein, the Hollywood's managing director was born in Northeast and attended local schools. He learned the theater business with his father Louis at the Faust and Dale theaters in St.Paul. Many other theaters that opened in the 30s were remodeled structures, but the Hollywood was built specifically as a theater. It was designed by architects Jack Liebenberg and Seeman Kaplan in the zig-zag Art Deco style which grew out of a new fascination with the speed and materials of the machine age. Because of the extensive decorating budget; the Hollywood became an Art Deco masterpiece. The lobby contained an inlaid terrazzo floor in grey, yellow, black and pink geometric shapes. The inner lobby has a vaulted ceiling and the walls are highlighted with colored lighting from indented capitals. The original Hollywood marquee was removed in 1946 and in 1960 many changes were made. A new triangular marquee replaced the original one. In 1968, the Hollywood was listed in a directory of "Great American Movie Theaters" published by the National Trust for Historic Preservation Commission. They eventually designated the Hollywood as historic. Which means that any re-use of the building would have to preserve the original exterior and interior of the building. Now, the Hollywood Theater Preservation group is committed to purchasing the building and restoring it to an operational movie theater in its original elegance.

*Hollywood Theater 1936.*

# JAX CAFE

1928 University Avenue NE, is the original business of the Kozlak family empire, which includes Kozlak University Funeral Chapel, Jax in Golden Valley, and Kozlak's Royal Oak, Shoreview. Stanley Kozlak came to America when he was just seventeen and immediately began working at a sawmill on Nicollet Island. In 1881, he became an agent for the Cunard steamship line and escorted European groups, sometimes whole villages, from Poland, the Ukraine, and Slovakia to America. When Stan Kozlak erected a brick building in 1910 to house a furniture, hardware, and undertaking business, the property he chose was on the edge of town. But a community quickly developed around the business. Stan based his business solely on trust and never felt a need for a contract. Even after his death in 1916 at the age of 46, clients continued to pay their bills. Jax Cafe opened in 1933 at the end of prohibition and was expanded in 1943 by Joseph and Gertrude Kozlak. Today, a grand mahogany bar, waterfall, and trout stream by the backyard garden patio are the cafe's hallmarks. House specialties are choice beef, fresh seafood, and live lobster. The menu also includes fresh fish from Minnesota and Canada.

Summertime in Jax Old World Garden showing the live flamingos and a net full of fighting rainbow trout.

## JOHN ORTH BREWERY

1215 Marshall Street NE, began with a German immigrant who is credited with establishing a major Twin Cities industry. In 1850, John Orth produced the first beer made in Hennepin County and opened the second brewery in Minnesota. Water for the process came from an artesian well on the premises. A native of the Alsace region in Europe, Orth arrived in this country with knowledge of the industry acquired in both France and Germany. Orth owned racing horses, which were kept in the rear of the brewery building.

In 1887, Orth died and his son, John W. Orth, inherited the business. Shortly thereafter, the Orth Brewery merged with three others to form the Minneapolis Brewing and Malting Company, which later became Grain Belt Brewery. The company officers decided to operate from the Orth building, and just one year later, built the structure that stands today at this address. The building's unusual Romanesque architecture led to its designation as a historical landmark in 1977. Orth left the brewing business in 1893 for a real estate enterprise.

*Orth's Brewery 1880.*

## KRAMARCZUK
## EAST EUROPEAN DELI

215 East Hennepin Avenue, remains in the center of Northeast's business district. Vasil Kramarczuk opened his first store in Pidhaytsi, a small town in the western Ukraine. When the Bolsheviks invaded his homeland, Vasil escaped to Germany. The quintessential entrepreneur, Vasil owned several businesses including a fabric store, a candy shop, a bookstore, and a dry goods mercantile, as well as a meat shop and restaurant before moving to Northeast Minneapolis. He and his wife saved $5,000 and opened up a sausage company at 2210 Marshall Street NE. When his partner disappeared with all the money, Vasil simply made plans to begin again. With the money he made as a landlord and cash he received from relatives, he started the William Kramarczyk Sausage Company in the 1950s. The cafeteria-style restaurant and Eastern European deli still remain popular among downtown office workers, and business at lunchtime is brisk.

## LITTLE JACK'S STEAKHOUSE

201 Lowry Avenue NE, opened in 1932. Josephine Reshetar and her husband Jack began this steakhouse in an 1890 building. Josephine's father-in-law Frank Reshetar, a Russian immigrant, taught her to make the Eastern European specialties that won so many awards throughout the years. A *Saturday Evening Post* article written in the 1940s distinguished Josephine as one of the few female restaurant owners and chefs in the United States. Josephine's two sons took over the restaurant in 1970, and the restaurant maintains its distinction as the oldest family-owned restaurant in Minnesota. Today, Little Jack's specializes in hardy American fare like steaks and seafood but continues to serve ethnic cuisine once a month and for special holidays.

*Irene Koniar and Florence Luniewski in front of Little Jacks 1940s.*

## KRAWCZYK'S SAUSAGE COMPANY

125 Lowry Avenue NE, earned a reputation for fine Polish sausage and barbecued ham from its 1913 beginnings. The oldest member of the family, Grandpa Mitchelslaus, came from Sandomeish, Poland. He once peddled the meat from house-to-house by horse and buggy. Recipes used at the sausage company had been perfected through the generations. A smokehouse, wooden barrels, mixing tubs, and a hand-cranked sausage stuffer on the premises guaranteed homemade goodness. On religious holidays, people would line up outside the store to purchase food baskets to be blessed at the church services. Before the business was sold in the early 1980s, many loyal clients had patronized the deli for fifty years.

## M. A. GEDNEY PICKLE COMPANY

began in 1880 at the corner of Lowry Avenue and Pacific Street. An adventurer at heart, Matthias Anderson Gedney served in the Navy, gathered gold dust in California, rescued seamen in distress on Lake Michigan, and brought corn to the starving Irish population during the famine. He lived in New York near Central Park, Evanston, Illinois, and LaCrosse, Wisconsin before settling in Minnesota. To create a prosperous business, Gedney encouraged farmers to sign contracts for their produce, an early form of the now prevalent commercial farming practices. Under Gedney's son, Isadore, the company continued its steady growth and, by 1923, the company owned three plants and 50 salting houses in Wisconsin and Minnesota and employed 250 people. In 1958, the company moved to Chaska because of increasing space needs. And by the 1970s, Gedney procured over 2,000 contracts with farmers. Gedney markets its product as the "Minnesota pickle" and remains family-owned.

# MISSES JOHNSON'S DEPARTMENT STORE

2027 Central Avenue, was named for the sibling owners, Freda, Ellen, and Olga Johnson. The department store began as a simple millinery establishment. But when the business proved very successful, the three sisters moved the enterprise to a larger building on Twenty-second Street and Central Avenue. Eventually, their store became the largest women's department store on the east side.

*Millinery Department of Misses Johnson's Department Store 1915.*

## NORTHERN PUMP COMPANY

4800 East River Road, resulted from the 1913 merger of Northern Fire Apparatus Company and the Theodore Pagel Pump Company. In 1928, John Hawley, Jr. purchased ownership of the company with the $100,000 he had earned for various inventions and ideas and, under his direction, the company flourished. Hawley predicted World War II after a European visit and began company preparations upon his return to the states. Hawley's foresight along with his reputation for being ahead of schedule, sometimes by two years, garnered many government contracts. His innovative ideas, such as supplying workers with low-cost meals, permitting unlimited overtime, providing interest-free emergency loans, making arrangements for transportation to work by private streetcars, and staffing an on-site hospital, factored heavily in the company's overall efficiency. Always a visionary, Hawley prepared the company for peace just as he did for war and diversified its holdings. By investing in oil and agriculture, Hawley maintained a healthy business. Today, the Fridley company employs about 1500 people, which is about one third of the wartime high.

## NORTHERN STATES POWER

3100 Marshall Street NE, formerly known as Minnesota Electric Light and Electric Motive Power Company, helped insure Minneapolis' status as a flour milling giant. Since Father Hennepin's discovery of St. Anthony Falls, enterprising businessmen recognized the falls as an enormous source of energy, and worked to harness and preserve nature's force. Minnesota's original power company, Minnesota Brush Electric, formed in 1881. The hydroelectric plant built at the bottom of the falls began operation in September of 1882, and the company landed the first streetlight contract for $200. The present-day Riverside plant replaced the original structure after it burned down in 1911. Over the years, multiple additions to the building led to the vast plant covering two city blocks. Visitors can discover more about the history of this groundbreaking company by touring the Heritage Hall museum at the Riverside station.

## NORTHRUP, KING & COMPANY

1500 Jackson Street NE, began in 1884 with two young men from the East establishing a seed house. In December of that year, the two partners issued their first price list for "Polar Brand Seeds". Jesse Northrup and Charles Braslan chose Minnesota for their enterprise for two reasons. First, they believed northern climates produced hardier vegetables and, consequently, more robust seeds. Second, they envisioned the great agricultural potential of the Midwest and decided Minneapolis would be an ideal distribution point for their product. The partners predicted correctly and, during the next ten years, operations moved three times to meet the needs of the expanding business. By 1889, the company had over 1800 acres under contract. During its first years the company weathered bankruptcy, fire, and volatile agricultural economies. The Jackson Street building closed in 1986 when a company in Tennessee purchased the packet seed division. Corporate headquarters in Golden Valley still produces farm seeds.

## NORTHWESTERN CASKET

1707 Jefferson Street NE, first opened In the 1880s. The business has changed tremendously over the years. In the '30s and '40s, the company employed 100 people, most living in the Northeast area. During World War II, almost all of the caskets had to be made of cloth-covered wood, as steel was saved for military purposes. At one time, wooden caskets were the only product but embroidery and tailoring of casket linings has become the primary business as the company continues to serve funeral directors in the five-state area. Currently owned and managed by William Shields, David Koll, Bob Berny, and Robert Bishop, the company employs about thirty-one people. So, the tradition of excellence continues in the craftsmen studios of Northwestern Casket.

## SCHERER BROTHERS LUMBER COMPANY

Ninth Avenue NE at the Mississippi River, began when siblings Clarence and Munn decided to give up farming. The brothers bought half-interest in a deadhead business in 1929 for $240. Deadheaders use long poles with metal ends to loosen stray pieces of lumber lodged in the soft river mud. No longer prime lumber, this wood sufficed for framing and sheathing. Slabs of bark from the water-logged lumber were sold as firewood, while merchants used the sawdust made from the bark as insulation in ice houses. World War II brought prosperity to the company, as defense contractors needed all shapes and sizes of lumber. Later, the postwar housing boom contributed to even faster growth. The brothers and, later, their sons built a business specializing in providing quality building products to small contractors. This thriving business continues to operate in the same Northeast location and has expanded to Shakopee and Arden Hills.

## SENTYRZ STORE

1612 Second Street NE, dates back to 1910. Stanley Sentyrz purchased the store from a man named Harenza in 1923. Stanley also owned funeral cars and even a Jitney bus, so-called because a ride cost five cents or a "jitney". Walt Sentyrz, his son, began to manage the store in 1956 after his mother died. Over the years, he has acquired a reputation as the unofficial historian of the area. Walt Jr. began managing the store in 1985. Store specialties include kielbasa and Polska synka, a Polish ham. Butchers use old world recipes for smoked ham, jerky, and Polish lunch meat. Gene Krawczyk of Krawczyk's Meat Market still works at the deli counter part time. Blackey's Bakery delivers ethnic breads, and customers can purchase the Dzienik Polski, a Polish newspaper. The store stocks nine different Polish hard candies and fudge and the liquor department sells imported Polish alcohol.

## SOO LINE RAILROAD

2800 Central Avenue NE, history can be traced back to the 1880s. At that time, Chicago interests controlled freight rates, which many Minneapolis business owners, dependent upon this transportation route, thought arbitrarily high. So financial leaders organized a competing transportation system. Names associated with the "Soo" include Thomas Lowry, William D. Washburn, and Charles A. Pillsbury. Unlike the early land grant railroads and their rail barons, private funds built the Soo. Instead of heading east through Chicago, the Soo went via Sault Ste. Marie and continued to the Atlantic coast on the Canadian Pacific System. Later, connections to North and South Dakota and north through Minnesota brought wheat from Canadian provinces to the mills and distributors of Minneapolis and St. Paul. From its inception, the railroad has been considered a Minneapolis company, with operations based at Shoreham Yard in Northeast. Built in 1887, the yard quickly became the major freight car repair shop for the railroads. As one of the earliest and largest employers in the Northeast neighborhood, the Soo played an important part in building the community. Certain proof of the railroad's influence on the economy of Northeast occurred on Soo Line paydays, when merchants in the Central Avenue business district did a thriving business. The yard still operates today, but the Soo shops building on Central Avenue was torn down in 1995.

*Soo Line Streetscene.*

## SUN DRIVE-IN

2951 Central Avenue, was "Home of the Famous Sunburger." Alfred Sorterbeer built the original structure in 1947. Warren Nelson purchased the property in 1956, remodeled it, and turned it into one of the hottest spots in the Twin Cities. During the era when Detroit boomed and Americans were reluctant to leave their cars, drive-ins allowed customers to order their meals right from their front seats. Carhops brought the food directly to their hungry clients from the small red and white building. On Friday and Saturday evenings, teens usually monopolized the drive-in, before and after drag racing and cruisin' along Central Avenue. The evening specials were "the Sundowner," which consisted of a Sunburger, Fries and a beverage for $1.45 and "the Back Seat Special" of a hamburger and a milkshake for just 85 cents. Eventually, the drive-in fad dwindled and, with only a very few exceptions, most drive-in food establishments closed along with their parallel phenomena, the drive-in movie. The Sun Drive-In succumbed along with its compatriots and the building was destroyed in the 1980s. Today, a Tom Thumb convenience store stands where guys with ducktails and girls with poodle skirts used to meet. But movies like *American Graffiti* preserve the memories and culture of this time.

## SURDYK'S LIQUOR STORE

303 East Hennepin Avenue, opened in 1934 when prohibition ended. Joseph Surdyk came from Poland in the late 1800s as a young man of eighteen. He found work as a streetcar conductor upon his arrival but quickly became a business owner. He already owned a grocery store on Thirteenth Avenue and Fourth Street when he purchased the liquor store. Surdyk's continues to specialize in beers, wines, and cheeses with great attention to the products from the popular microbreweries, like James Page beer, which is made on Thirteenth Avenue in Northeast Minneapolis.

## THE TOWN PUMP

801 Marshall Street, was named for the old-fashioned pump in front of the business, which attracted people far and wide for the purity of its water. The tavern, established in 1891, was first owned by the Gluek's Brewery. In 1914, the building's venue changed when owners opened a boarding house that included a coffee house and ice cream parlor. During Prohibition, Stan Cossie purchased the business and continued operating it as a coffee house. Joseph Mancino and his brother, Russell, bought the bar in 1964 with Joseph becoming the sole owner by 1971. During Joseph's tenure, customers lined up for the daily spaghetti and meatball specials. Clients often purchased his spaghetti sauce by the quart. In the '60s, the bar became popular with the Grain Belt Brewery crowd. Joseph continued the Italian tradition of feeding the poor and provided free dinners on every holiday. After his death in 1992, Todd Parker bought the bar. And although he took out the original booths, Parker decided to keep the 1907 mahogany bar, which he just refinished this past year.

## UKRAINIAN GIFT SHOP

2422 Central Avenue, is located on the main business thoroughfare in Northeast. Luba Perchyshyn and her mother Marie Procai began this enterprise in their living room in 1947. The business is best known for the colorful eggs, called "pysanka," that are created, displayed, and sold in the shop. These eggs have both religious connotations and personal meanings to Ukrainians. Marie began making pysanka when she first arrived in America at the beginning of this century and suffered from a severe case of homesickness. To counteract her loneliness, she began dying eggs by soaking crepe paper in boiling water and etching designs in the shell with a tool made from a shoelace tip. Luba carries on her mother's traditions and several of her eggs have become part of White House displays.

## WILCOX MOTOR CAR COMPANY

Tenth & Marshall Street NE, began as a manufacturer of motor vehicles with the introduction of the 1907 Wolfe. Customers could choose between touring, baby tonneau, or "gentleman's roadster" models, all selling for $1,500. John Finley Wilcox established the business after owning a sash and door factory in the late 1800s. Upon the death of his father, Harry E. Wilcox managed the company. Responding to new transportation needs between cities, the company began manufacturing trucks and, eventually, truck and bus production eclipsed the automobile lines. Carl H. Will purchased the business in 1926 and, shortly thereafter, records of the company disappear.

*Tractors in front of Wilcox Truck Co. 1915.*

*Pete Guzy holding his son Pete Jr. in about 1960. Pete Jr. went on to become one of the better punters for the Edison Tommies.*

# 5 After a Hard Day's Work

## Northeast Sports

**By Stew Thornley**

Northeast Minneapolis produced more than its share of outstanding athletes. Some even advanced to major-league levels. Many people have speculated on the reason. The Northeast culture, which fostered strong values, high standards, and a spirit of competition continues to be a place where residents instruct and value spending time with both their own and other kids. Naturally a deep connection developed between the families and their love of sports. Large families often supplied enough members to round out their own basketball squad or even a baseball nine. The lives of many Northeast children revolved around sports through school, park board, and church teams. Nuns and priests, in full garb, weren't shy about getting involved in a baseball game to demonstrate the finer points. Even picnics and family get-togethers had athletic activities as their main attraction.

"Northeast Minneapolis has always played a prominent role in the field of sports and recreation, thanks to the combined efforts of our schools, churches, parks, settlement houses, and business and professional men. Through their efforts, they offered opportunities to young and old, girls as well as boys, to compete in sports and recreational activities of their own choosing and, as a result, many young people reached the heights in professional, semi-professional, and amateur athletics." That assessment of Northeast sports notoriety came from Pete Guzy, forever the shining symbol of athletic greatness in Northeast Minneapolis.

### PETE GUZY

Guzy is well remembered as a teacher and coach at Edison High School for more than thirty-five years. His alma mater was East High School, which served all Minneapolis students on the east side of the Mississippi River from 1899 to 1924, until the opening of Edison and Marshall High Schools in Northeast and Southeast Minneapolis, respectively. While at East High, Guzy earned ten letters in baseball, basketball, and football, serving as captain on all three teams. On the baseball diamond, he was truly outstanding, leading the East Cardinals to their first City Conference championships in 1921 and 1922. He was a terror on the mound and no slouch with the bat. In his junior season in 1921, he compiled a .423 batting average while racking up a 7–0 record as a pitcher and nearly single-handedly taking the Cardinals to the championship. Pete won his fifth game of the season, a 2–1 win over South High on Tuesday, May 17th. Strikeout totals in double figures were not at all unusual for the diminutive righthander. On May 10th he fanned twenty North High batters and followed that up three days later with a 14 strikeout performance against Central, a team that featured the sons of two former Minneapolis Miller stars, Otis Clymer and Jimmie Williams. The Central game drew a crowd of more than 4,000 fans, typical of the type of support East High received from its boosters that year.

In 1921 championship came down to a game between East and Central on Tuesday, May 31st. For the second time in a row, Guzy struck out fourteen Pioneer batters, finishing with a four hitter and a 1–0 victory to give the Cardinals their first ever championship in baseball.

East High made it two in a row in 1922 as Guzy once again compiled a record of seven wins and no losses. Guzy was the first recipient of the Mark Hamilton Award, a trophy presented to the school for its top athlete by the Mark Hamilton American Legion Post. (After East High closed, the award continued at Marshall High School until that school closed in 1982.) Guzy's athletic prowess was recognized not just at East, but throughout the City Conference; in 1922 he was voted the best athlete for the entire city of Minneapolis.

Guzy attended the University of Minnesota where he played both football and baseball, being named to the All Big Ten team in the latter sport in 1925. Upon graduation, he began his legendary career in coaching. He started out at Faribault High School, fifty miles south of the Twin Cities, then took a coaching position at Superior High School in Superior, Wisconsin. One of his top athletes was Tuffy Leemans, who is now a member of the Pro Football Hall of Fame.

During the time he was coaching, Pete stayed active as an athlete. He had a brief fling in professional baseball, pitching for the Duluth Dukes in the Northern League. He also played semi-pro baseball for many years and was a top bowler in the area, with a consistent average of over 190.

One of Guzy's biggest thrills as an athlete came in 1935, just as he prepared to begin his coaching tenure at Edison High School. Guzy pitched for the Minneapolis Police Team in a Labor Day game against St. Paul Police at Nicollet Park, the home of the Minneapolis Millers. This game featured a barnstorming appearance by Babe Ruth, who had retired from major league baseball just a few months earlier. To keep things equal, the Babe played one half game with each team, and although he didn't give the fans what they were hoping for—a home run—he did manage a double in four at bats. Meanwhile, Guzy pitched the entire game for the Minneapolis Police and struck out eighteen batters, including the Babe.

Guzy coached football at Edison from 1935 through 1966, with an overall record of 132–84–20. Six times during his reign—1938, 1939, 1942, 1948, 1949, and 1956, the Tommies either won or tied for the City Conference championship. They had a perfect 7–0 record in 1942 and 1948 and won the Twin City Championship game both years. In 1944 Guzy began coaching baseball and continued through the 1971 season. Edison won the city, region, and state championship in 1949.

In 1983, Guzy became the first inductee into the Edison High School Hall of Fame. At that time, a scholarship in his name was also created. Since 1984, a number of deserving Edison student athletes have been able to pursue opportunities in higher education, thanks to the Pete Guzy scholarship fund.

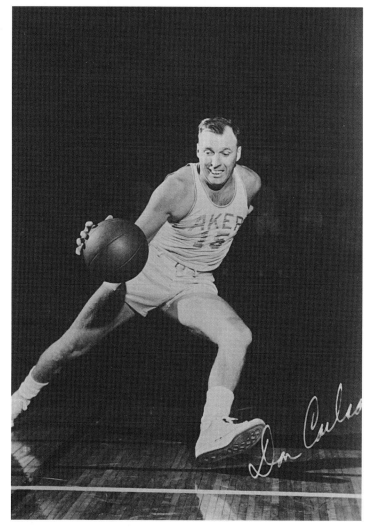

*Don Carlson.*

## DON "SWEDE" CARLSON

"You talk pressure. I'll tell you what pressure was: growing up a Swede in Northeast Minneapolis." Those are the words of Don "Swede" Carlson, who often laughs about how unusual it was in this area to have a name like Carlson.

Carlson was a member of the 1937 state championship Edison basketball team as a senior, and also played football for Pete Guzy as well as baseball. Following high school, Carlson played basketball for the Minnesota Gophers, then spent four years in the Air Force during World War II. Upon his discharge, he hooked up with an Amateur Athletic Union (AAU) in Kansas City sponsored by the M & O Cigar Company. This league included the Phillips Oilers, sponsored by Phillips Petroleum Company, which had seven foot Bob Kurland at center. Kurland was one of the greatest players of all time. Playing before defensive goaltending was outlawed, he easily swatted away shots descending toward the basket. Carlson remembers how difficult it was playing against Kurland: "You'd fake and fake and fake, try to get him to move, then shoot quickly." While in Kansas City, Carlson got a call from Harold Olsen, the coach of the Chicago Stags in the new Basketball Association of America. Olsen asked if he would be interested in joining the Stags and playing in a professional league.

"I thought it would be a better deal for my family," says Swede, "So that's what we did."

The Stags made it all the way to the league championship before losing to the Philadelphia Warriors and the great Joe Fulks. "What a shooter he was," says Carlson.

Carlson was voted the Stags' Most Valuable Player

in 1946–47. Even though he was barely over six feet tall, Carlson played forward. His job wasn't to score but to serve as a defensive specialist. "In those days, teams looked for a player who could hold someone down. I would pick the best shooting guy on the other team and stick to him all game."

One of Carlson's teammates on the Stags was Tony Jaros, another great athlete from Northeast Minneapolis. In 1947, Carlson and Jaros became the first members of the Minneapolis Lakers of the National Basketball League. Local businessmen created the Lakers when they purchased the Detroit Gems, who were on the verge of collapse. None of the players came with the team when they transferred to Minneapolis. Considering that the Gems had posted a record of 4–40 with the talent they had during the 1946–47 season, it wasn't surprising that the new owners would prefer to start from scratch in building the team. The first move they made was to purchase the contracts of Don Carlson and Tony Jaros from the Chicago Stags. Carlson was in the starting lineup for the first game ever played by the Minneapolis Lakers, on November 1, 1947. Not only that, Swede won the game with a basket in the final seconds of the contest, giving the Lakers a 49–47 victory over the Oshkosh All-Stars.

The Lakers built their team well, so well that they went on to win the National Basketball League title in 1947–48. The team included Jim Pollard, a former All-American at Stanford University, and George Mikan, the greatest player in basketball at the time. Carlson was the Lakers third leading scorer, behind Mikan and Pollard.

In 1948 the Lakers changed leagues switching to the Basketball Association of America, the league that included Carlson's former team, the Chicago Stags. Once again, the Lakers won the league championship. The Basketball Association of America merged with the National Basketball League, creating the National Basketball Association in 1949. The Lakers once again finished first, winning the 1949–50 championship, their third title in their third league in three years.

Carlson played the 1950–51 season with the Baltimore Bullets and Washington Capitols before retiring from pro ball. He stayed active in athletics, however, coaching a variety of sports for fifteen years at Columbia Heights High School. When the athletic director's job opened up, he moved into the position. Before finally retiring in 1985 he supervised twenty-four different sports.

## TONY JAROS

Possibly the greatest all around athlete in the history of the Minneapolis City Conference, Tony Jaros followed in the footsteps of Swede Carlson in high school, college and eventually in the professional ranks. After graduating from Edison in 1940, three years after Carlson, Jaros then enrolled at the University of Minnesota. He played basketball on the Gopher freshman squad before enlisting in the military.

He played on an all GI team while in the service. In 1943, while stationed in Battle Creek, Michigan, he took some leave and joined a team from Shakopee. The Rock Springs Sparklers played in the World Professional Tournament in Chicago. The Sparklers, which included another top Northeast athlete, Willie Warhol, won their first game before losing to the

*Tony Jaros.*

Washington, D.C. Bears, an all black team that went on to win the tournament.

After the war, Jaros returned to the University of Minnesota and resumed his athletic career. After a year, he ventured into the pros, not just in basketball but in baseball, as well.

Jaros signed with the Minneapolis Millers and played baseball in their organization, first with the St. Cloud Rox of the Northern League and then briefly with the Millers in 1946. He also played with Sioux City and Omaha in the St. Louis Cardinals chain. After his professional days were over, he continued playing baseball in semi-pro leagues, including the Faribault Lakers in the vaunted Southern Minnesota League.

Jaros' athletic career was especially challenging because he also played professional basketball. Along with Swede Carlson, he played with the Chicago Stags during the first year of the Basketball Association of America. In 1947 the two athletes eventually signed with the new Minneapolis Lakers franchise in the National Basketball League.

One of Jaros' biggest moments with the Lakers came in April of 1950. The Lakers finished the regular season with a 51–17 record, tied with the Rochester Royals for first place in the NBA's Central Division. A playoff game was held in Rochester to break the first-place tie. Minneapolis trailed by six points with just three minutes left to play, but battled back to tie the game. With just three seconds left, Jaros threw a long shot that sailed through the basket to give the Lakers a 78–76 win. Jaros said that one shot bought him another year in pro basketball and his team went on to win their third straight league championship. He played a total of four seasons with the Lakers and was George Mikan's roommate when the team was on the road.

Because the Lakers were invariably in the playoffs, their basketball season extended into April, so Jaros often had to report late for the baseball season. At a rate of $70 a game, the Southern Minny League, with its semi-pro status, actually paid Jaros more than he earned playing for the Lakers.

Even after the conclusion of his playing days were done, Jaros remained a Northeast legend. He opened a landmark that still bears his name—Tony Jaros' River Gardens. The original River Gardens, which he opened in 1951, was on 8th and Marshall, in the building that now houses Elsie's Bowling Alley. Ten years later he moved the business to its current location on Lowry Avenue and Marshall Streets and set up living quarters above the bar.

Jaros attended numerous reunions and functions of the Minneapolis Lakers. On April 18, 1995, four days before he died, Tony got together with his former teammates for one last time at the Target Center. The Timberwolves held a reception to honor Vern Mikkelsen and John Kundla, Tony's former teammate and coach, respectively, upon their election into the Basketball Hall of Fame. At the reception, George Mikan took a moment to sit down and chat with his former roommate, the man he called "Yaros." The ex-Lakers were brought onto the floor at half-time of the Timberwolves game and introduced individually. The loudest applause went to Kundla and Mikkelsen, the new inductees into the Hall of Fame, as well as to Mikan. But Tony got his share of cheers when he was introduced. It was apparent that area sports fans still remembered Tony Jaros, one of the best athletes ever from any part of Minneapolis.

## Other Northeast greats

### J. SAM MISENCIK

mixed a rich ethnic heritage with a love for sports while growing up in a duplex on Twenty-fifth Street and University Avenue. Even though he was only five feet-two inches tall, Misencik was an all-city basketball player at Edison. Also known as one of the "best all-around park athletes" in the area, Misencik played second base for the Pillsbury House softball team for many years.

An outstanding golfer, Misencik won many local tournaments and became director of the Minnesota Public Golf Association and president of the Gross Golf Course.

In addition to participating in sports as an athlete, Misencik remained active in officiating roles. A softball umpire for many years, he began timing a number of sports in 1951. He served as official timekeeper for the Minneapolis Lakers and later performed this job for the Minnesota Muskies of the American Basketball Association, the Minnesota Fillies of the Women's Professional Basketball Team, and for games played locally by the Harlem Globetrotters.

Despite all his athletic achievements, people of Northeast knew Misencik as "Sam the Banker." He worked for many years for Northwestern National Bank, retiring as vice president in 1977. He didn't retire completely, but came back to serve as a part-time consultant at the branch on Central Avenue. Because of his fluency in Ukrainian, Polish, Slovakian, and

*Sam J. Misencik.*

Russian, he worked with the diverse population in Northeast and served many of the older residents who didn't speak English. He continued dispensing banking advice and swapping sports stories up until his death in September of 1994.

## ZIG BISHOP

one of the great promoters, managers, and coaches for sports ranging from softball and baseball to basketball and football was named America's Most Active Sportsman in 1954.

"Sports was all there was," said Bishop, speaking of the period in which he grew up in a 1982 interview for *Mpls.-St. Paul* magazine. "If you couldn't find a sponsor, you held a little raffle to buy your shirts. In the winter, we packed the Northeast Neighborhood House. They couldn't get the doors open fast enough before we'd be in there fighting to get a ball. On Sunday, you had to get to Bottineau Park in Northeast early in the morning or you'd never get on a field."

Born in 1908 Bishop moved from scrapping on the sandlots as a youth to overseeing the activities of others. He sponsored Bishop's Jersey Ice Cream softball teams, winners of three national championships.

*Zig Bishop and his Jersey Ice Cream Softball team 1950s.*

Later, he coached amateur basketball teams. The team's rosters included John Kundla—who would later become coach of the Minneapolis Lakers and who would be elected to the Basketball Hall of Fame in 1995 and Harry Peter "Bud" Grant, who played two seasons for the Minneapolis Lakers but is better remembered as the coach who guided the Minnesota Vikings to four Super Bowls and is now a member of the Pro Football Hall of Fame.

When amateur sports reigned in Northeast, Zig Bishop was the king of them all.

## ARNIE SIMSO

is remembered best for his long association with the game of kittenball. This fast-pitch softball game was actually invented in Northeast Minneapolis in 1908. Simso's name appeared on Wheaties box tops in the 1940s proclaiming him one of the nation's top softball pitchers. His ability to change speeds on his pitches, as well as a talent for making his pitches rise, drop, and curve, made them difficult to hit.

Before taking up the sport of kittenball at the age of 23, Simso was a star athlete at East and Edison. He graduated in 1925 after earning high-school letters in tennis, football, basketball, baseball, and hockey. From there, he attended Carleton College in Northfield, playing basketball for Ozzie Cowles, who would later coach at Dartmouth and the University of Minnesota.

After his high school and collegiate days were over, Simso moved to kittenball. After twelve years of being the best in the game, Simso hung up his glove but not his love of athletics. He eventually became manager of the Bowl-O-Mart in Apache Plaza.

*Arnie Simso holding his plaque for Edison Hall of Fame*

## MARTY ROLEK

a 1932 Edison graduate, was a college All-American and the star player on the Minnesota Gophers 1937 basketball team, which tied for the Big Ten Championship.

*Marty Rolek.*

*Butch Nash.*

## BUTCH NASH

was a fullback on the Edison gridiron, guard on the basketball court, and first baseman on the diamond who became well known across the state during his forty years of coaching the Minnesota Gophers football team.

*In 1900 the new Eastside High became the first high school in East Minneapolis. It was located on Central Avenue be-tween 4th St. and University Ave. SE where the Eastgate Shopping Center is today. From 1917 till 1924, East High grew from 1,200 to 1,910 pupils. A part of old East, both students and faculty moved to Edison when it was complete in 1922. In 1924 the remainder of East were transferred to John Marshall High. These two schools continued the old East spirit. The old building was used for a boy's Vocational school until 1939.*

Many Northeasters played in the major leagues in a variety of sports. Clayton Tonnemaker played center for the Green Bay Packers after an outstanding multisport career at Edison and later at the University of Minnesota. Tonnemaker made the All-American team in 1949 and is now a member of the College Football Hall of Fame.

Walt Edwards went on to play in the Canadian Football League while Floyd Jaszewski and Bob Wetoska played in the National Football League. Jaszewski became part of the Detroit Lions and Wetoska teamed up with the Chicago Bears. In the 1940s and 1950s, Paul Mitchell played with the Los Angeles Dons in the All-American Football Conference and the New York Yankees.

There were the many longtime Northeast coaches who taught their crafts at both East and Edison high schools: Louie Lopata, Ray Parkins, Harry Miller, Guil Parsons, Niles Schultz, Ben Liemohn, Homer Pile, and Mike Doyle.

In baseball, there was Pete Turgeon enjoying a cup of coffee with the Chicago Cubs in 1923 and Charley Walters taking a few turns on the mound for the Minnesota Twins in 1969 before going on to greater fame as a sports columnist with the *St. Paul Pioneer Press*.

Like Sam Misencik, Northeast athletes often became well known in other endeavors after their playing days. Walt Dziedzic served as a longtime city councilmember representing Northeast Minneapolis. Harold Kalina became a judge and Wayne Courtney was elected mayor of Edina.

East and Edison are not the only two high schools associated with Northeast Athletics. De La Salle High School, located on Nicollet Island, continues to draw students from the entire city, but a large portion are students from Northeast. In addition to the schools, the neighborhood centers often sponsor athletic activities. For instance the Northeast Neighborhood House hosted the All Nations Basketball Tournament. Then of course, city parks like Logan, Sheridan, Bottineau, Marshall Terrace, and Jackson Square allowed young Northeasters to frolic and hone their skills as they hoped one day to be able to add to Northeast's athletic legacy.

It's impossible to chronicle all the athletes, not to mention all the different places they played. The Edison Sports Hall of Fame does recognize those who brought fame and honor to the neighborhood. Although times have changed there are those who still remember the days of great Northeast Sports Glory when no one could beat the teams from Northeast.

*Walt Dziedzic and Pete Guzy.*

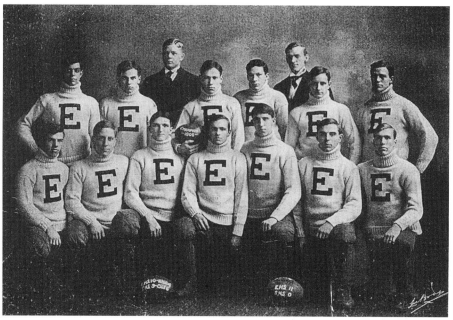

*East High Football Champs 1906.*

*Twin City Football champs in front of Edison 1942.*

*Marshall-Edison Baseball game 1925.*

THE BASKET BALL TEAM, 1906

Way (Manager)

Kendall     Cockburn     Eberhard     Hawley
          Greene       Elliott        Werring
                Brand

*East High Basketball champions 1906.*

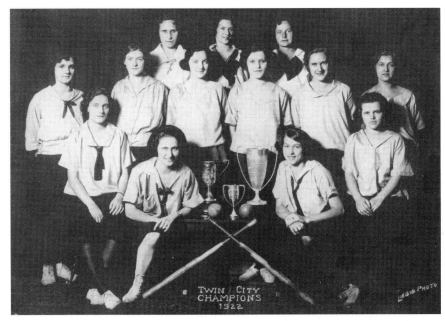

*Twin City Kittenball Champions 1922.*

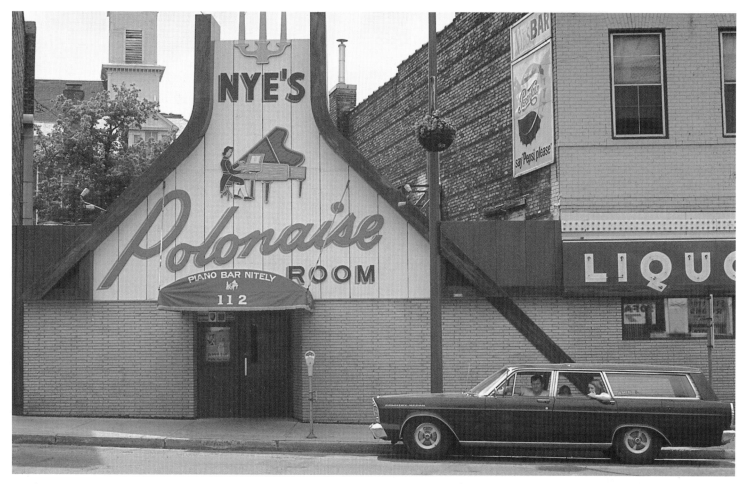

*Nye's Bar and Polonaise Room served as a harness shop from 1905 to 1920, then converted to a hotel in the 1920s. In 1955 it became Nye's Bar. The smaller building connecting the harness shop and the old tavern was built in 1964.*

# Al's Place

**By Don Boxmeyer**
*St. Paul Pioneer Press:* March 3, 1991

Al Nye had serious doubts about his future in the restaurant business only once, very early in his long career. That's when the gang from the lutefisk plant across the street would slosh in for lunch, pushing his less fragrant clients to the limits of their allegiance.

"I didn't know what to do with the guys from Ranheim Fish Co. over on Main Street," Al says. "They liked to come for a few beers at noon, but they smelled so bad, I was losing all my other customers, I couldn't sleep at night wondering how I was going to tell the boys they couldn't come in anymore."

Then, the angel that must have been watching out for Al Nye and his Polonaise Room all these years took over. The big, old lutefisk plant in North Minneapolis burned down one night—and within a couple of years, Al says, all detectable traces of the operation were gone.

Al Nye, now in his 70s, would not become a victim to renewal, progress or pretense. He never made the mistake of getting fancy.

"I worked with the production crew at the old Coca-Cola Bottling Co. around the corner," recalls Jim Stevenson, a long-time friend of Al Nye. "We hung around the Huddle Bar because it was a pretty lively place—until the owners remodeled and decided to upgrade the clientele. One night, we had to slip into sports coats and neckties to get in. Imagine that: a bunch of guys in Coca-Cola coveralls and rubber boots wearing dinner jackets. That lasted about three nights. We came over to Al's and never left."

The Huddle Bar is gone now. But Nye's splendid little congregation of Polish dining rooms—the Polonaise Room, the Chopin Room and the Count Pulaski Room—still shares a block with the oldest church in Minneapolis, Our Lady of Lourdes, which dates back to 1857 and which for generations has sold its trademark meat pie as a take-out item.

Nye's 41 year-old restaurant—where nothing much ever changes, either—is one of the hottest spots in Minneapolis, catering to neighborhood old-timers, a loyal following from as far away as France, and a new, younger, Metropolitan crowd who, says one of Al Nye's bartenders, are "just tired of the loud music at other joints. We're laid back."

Behind this calm, solid, historic and unchanging buffer lurk the colorful remnants of a community that is not big on urban change. Kramarczuk Sausage Co. and bakery, Surdyk's liquors and Zelenyuk Shoes & Leather Co. still do business just north across the river from the Minneapolis Loop.

"Nordeast ain't into festive retailing," says Bob Perrizo, an artist and public-relations executive who is one of Nye's regulars. "Just how many loon candles does anyone need?"

Al Nye came into all this back in 1950, when he bought

a long, narrow beer joint with a big front window and a row of high-backed booths along the wall nearest the river. His neighbors were places like Fitz's Bar, the East Hennepin Cafe, Robert's Cafe and the Dog House.

Minneapolis had not yet gotten sophisticated enough to tear out all the old and replace it with the stunning new Riverplace, a red-brick monument to the machinations of bankruptcy court and shimmering restaurants that change their names and owners every time the ferns need watering. Some of his best customers, says Al with that amused, sort-of-perplexed, who-am-I-to-stop-them grin on his face, are employees of the glitzy new saloons and restaurants.

"Our prices are better," he says.

The keystone of Al Nye's empire is the Polonaise Room. That's French for Polish. Some cab driver—Al forgets his name—suggested it. People still come around thinking the place is a Polynesian supper club—a notion not dispelled by an exterior that for some reason resembles the bow of a Hawaiian war canoe coming out of the mist.

Al is no tinkerer, He has not tinkered with the original bar, other than to saw the tops off the booths, lower the ceilings 30 years ago and replace the bulbs in the warm little Grain Belt beer signs when necessary. Dozens of big silver trophies from slow-pitch softball tournaments line the walls on high shelves.

The venerable three-piece band that lights up the tavern with its polkas and fast waltzes has been playing on a tiny stage in the southeast corner of the room every Friday and Saturday night for at least 15 years, Al guesses. This is the Ruth Adams Band, so named because Ruth and her Chordovox accordion have been around longer than 61-year-old Tom Belkey on the sax and 76-year-old Al

Ophus, the drummer in the white shirt and tie, who croons "That's Amore" with just the right amount of pain and suffering. Ophus is the only vocalist in the group; Ruth Adams explains: "Baby Ruth don't sing."

It's in this long skinny New York-style tavern that you sense there might be something special going on at the Nye complex. Old men with big, hard knuckles—wearing dark suits, gold medallions under dress shirts open at the collar, and snug black fedoras—and their Saturday-night dates with beehive hairdos co-exist playfully with young people in their Dockers and Eddie Bauer jackets. This young crowd, wary of contrived fashion, pile in to where the authentic comes naturally. One young artist explains, "It's hip to not be hip."

The young crowd has discovered Okocim Polish beer in pint bottles, of which Al Nye now sells 12 to 14 cases a week, @ $2.75 per bottle with weekend music and $2.50 without.

"I've been reading Nye's menu for 30 years," says one of Al's regulars, WCCO Radio personality Dick Chapman. "At the bottom, it says 'Taste our Polish wine'—something called Nazdrowie. I asked for it once. Turns out they've never had any of the stuff."

Through a big pair of swinging doors in the tavern is the main dining room, with its gold-fleck Naugahyde banquettes and the big portrait of Chopin over the piano bar. This is the room Al opened in 1964, the first of three large dining rooms he added as more and more people discovered such things as pierogis, cabbage rolls, chili bonanzas and pork hocks with or without kraut.

Al has known about kraut for a long, long time—since he was a boy, stomping sauerkraut in 55 gallon barrels. He grew up in the Wisconsin woods, near Ladysmith, then boxed and lumberjacked for several years before coming to Minneapolis to become a welder and a foreman at the old Northern Pump Co.

Eventually, he bought his first tavern in South Minneapolis, and in 1950, wound up with the saloon on East Hennepin that came to be known as Nye's. Forty-one years later, Al Nye is still plowing his own parking lots at 6 A.M. after a snowfall—and he still supervises the secret construction of the signature sauerkraut in 20-gallon lots. Cooks and waitresses still bring samples of their coleslaw and kraut for his imprimatur before serving it to his customers.

His secrets, he says, are no secret. Show up for work early and stay late. Give the customer good food—and lots of it. Patiently consider all suggestions of change—before rejecting them. Be your own bouncer, if you've got the stuff. (Al, regulars say, has the stuff.) Don't let a fire slow you down.

The fire, on a Saturday morning in 1987, closed Nye's for several months and almost blinded Al, who subsequently received a cornea transplant and still suffers from the effects of the fire-extinguishing powder he caught in the face when trying to fight the kitchen blaze. During the time he was rebuilding, Al is proud to report, not one of his 63 employees lost any wages.

The Ruth Adams Trio is not the only fixture at Nye's. Marcie Anderson has been checking coats from 11 A.M. to 1 A.M. every day for 25 years, Lou Snyder has been playing at the main piano bar for 25 years. Al's daughter, Diane Bauer, is the longtime hostess. And his son, Rick, is a manager.

One recent Friday night when Lou Snyder wasn't at her spot behind the piano, George Griak sat in, passing the cordless microphone around to piano-bar veterans who needed very little coaxing to sing their versions of "Tenderly" and "I Wish You Love."

One old-timer sporting a topper that must have been styled by Lawn Boy grimaced his way through "My Funny Valentine." One slightly over-the-hill chanteuse sounded like an incoming missile, but Al, seated with some long-time customers from St. Paul, smiled and shrugged. Some things you just don't interfere with.

"Al gives his regular customers lots of room," Perrizo says. He recalls the pair of St. Paul characters who found a party of about 50 elderly women eating in Nye's basement dining room. The two waltzed right up to the head table and called the meeting to order.

"Welcome to the Altar and Rosary Society," one said. "I'm glad you could all be here today to hear Father Vincent's address on his favorite subject: the vows of celibacy."

His partner was well into describing the privations of his life before one of the women finally said, "We're not Altar and Rosary Society. We're retired Honeywell. But please continue."

"After that," Perrizo continues, "Al follows those two around whenever they start to wander."

One of the pair, a retired federal tax agent, was once at a large luncheon table where an official of the FBI was entertaining guests with stories about criminals. When the FBI agent was leaving, he discovered his pockets were full of silverware, salt and pepper shakers and ashtrays.

"We had a Christmas party over here one year, and one of the guests was a clergyman who kept telling Stu Voigt [retired Vikings tight end] how generous professional athletes usually were when it came time to buy lunch. Voigt didn't want to be impolite, so he kept the preacher in martinis for a couple of hours, until Santa Claus, who was a stripper, came in. The clergyman jumped up and kissed her."

Father Vincent again. Al Nye has learned to just shake his head at the antics, especially after being whoopee-cushioned by a priest for the 50th time.

"He's been sponsoring our bowling team now for 15 years, and we haven't brought a trophy home to him yet," says Jim Stevenson, the Coca-Cola bottler. "But he doesn't complain, and he's not abandoned us."

The team that never got off the ground was Al's sponsorship of a St. Paul bowling team, headed by Perrizo and some local newspaper and broadcasting types.

"Al was all for us, but we couldn't agree on a color for our shirts," Perrizo says. "There was in fact, only one thing we could agree on. We wanted to name our team, "Nye's guys finish last."

# Mayslack's: Roast Beef and Ethnic Trimmings.

*Mayslacks Polka Lounge 1428 NE 4th St.*

## By Brian Anderson

*Minneapolis Star & Tribune:* April 8, 1973

The young woman gingerly approached the menacing-looking figure behind the serving counter and stuck out her paper plate, daintily holding its edges with her hands.

"Palm up! Palm up!" said the bearded, Paul Bunyan-sized carver of the beef, letting the little lady know it takes a full hand to support a plate about to receive a man-sized sandwich.

Flustered by the big man's directions, the woman dropped one hand from the plate and held that hand out in front of her, palm up.

The beef server, without saying a word, plopped the hefty sandwich, with its juices running over, onto her out-stretched—and plateless—hand.

No one remembers what the woman's response was, and maybe it's just as well, but the guffaws from the woman's escort reportedly were heard all the way down to the Polish National Alliance Hall, a full block away.

The woman was, in the words of Stan Mayslack, the server and beef-sandwich king of Northeast Minneapolis, "a rookie." When the woman's escort gave Mayslack that information, Mayslack had the go-ahead to initiate her in the proper technique of handling a Mayslack beef sandwich.

"A lot of times I'll throw it (the sandwich) at the guy," said Mayslack, explaining his procedure for dealing with customers who don't hold their plates right.

"Oh, you don't throw them," corrected Mayslack's wife, Ann, who is more widely known as "Butch."

"Well I lay it on them," retorted her husband.

The scene of these beefy escapades is the famed Mayslack's Polka Lounge, a neighborhood bar at 1428 NE 4th St. whose customers come from neighborhoods hundreds of miles away.

"You ought to see our lunch lines," Mayslack said. "People from Japan, Taiwan, Australia, New Zealand—a lot of them can't even speak English."

At noon, Tuesday through Saturday, the attraction is the beef sandwich, made with tender loving care by the Mayslacks themselves, using a cooking recipe unknown to the rest of the world. They go through about 200 pounds of beef a day.

On assorted holidays, the attractions are celebrations that turn the bar from a Little Poland into a United Nations. St. Patrick's Day, Chinese New Year and the Russian New Year all are celebrated with appropriate fanfare, as are such notable occasions as the Polish Mardi Gras, Valentine's Day, Mother's Day and Bunny Day.

Mayslack pulls out all stops to set the appropriate mood for his parties. On the Chinese New Year, for example, he hangs Chinese lanterns from the ceiling, gives out straw coolie hats, umbrellas and noisemakers and advertises that a Polish polka band will play "Auld Lang Syne" in Chinese.

For the St. Patrick's Day party, he hangs shamrocks from the ceiling, serves green beer and green ice, dyes his beard and mustache green and sports a bright orange derby. The Irish celebration is usually the most popular of the year, with about 900 revelers taking part in the festivities between 8 P.M. and 1 A.M.

"It gets so crowded that night that girls can't even make it to the potty (room)," Mayslack said.

Mayslack was ill just before St. Patrick's Day this year, and thus didn't get all his Irish decorations put up in time. "But who knows," he said, "I may get the leprechauns up for Mother's Day instead."

Because of the Mayslack's propensity for hanging decorations from the ceiling, some people refer to the bar as "the hanging gardens."

"Sometimes we hang something up and let it hang for six, seven months," Mayslack said, noting that he didn't get the Chinese lanterns taken down until a couple of days before St. Patrick's Day. "People say we hang it until it falls down."

If it isn't the beef sandwich or the party nights that attract customers, it's the fact that Mayslack's, even on an ordinary day, is not your ordinary bar.

Signs proclaiming "Polish Power" and "No One Beats Mayslack's Meat," which has become the establishment's unofficial slogan, dot the walls and, as you might expect, hang from the ceiling.

At Mayslack's, pictures (some of them from the owner's former days as a professional wrestler) don't hang on the wall—they lean against it. You'd almost think that Jim Klobuchar's columns were a new wallpaper design, judging by the number of his columns which, extolling the virtues of the bar, are blown-up bigger-than-life and, of course, lean against the wall.

Three evenings a week a polka band takes to the stand, and the patrons—young and old—dance with a ferocity that make some of Mayslack's wrestling matches look like church cakewalks.

And presiding over the festivities each night is the 280-pound Mayslack, whose scowl and wrestling record have combined to tame the rowdiest of revelers.

"When I first came in here, there were a few young punks, but I told them from the start, 'You behave in here, no boo-boos, '" Mayslack said. "Once in a while you get a knucklehead who's really in the bag," he continues, "but when I walk by, they quiet down."

The Mayslacks—both of whom are Polish and were born and raised not far from their bar's location—have been running their Northeast landmark since 1955, when Mrs. Mayslack persuaded her husband to retire from the ring so that he could spend more time with her and their son.

Mayslack wrestled for 32 years before retiring, and many of his customers still recall his ring exploits. "People in the lunch line will say something about me being a dirty wrestler, but I tell them "No, I was just sneaky," he said.

Mayslack was promotion-conscious from the start, one of the reasons to which he attributes the bar's success. He began offering the beef sandwich as a 50-cent, post-football-game treat 15 years ago. Today more than 1,000 of the sandwiches, now priced at $2, are served during the 13½ hours they are sold each week.

Besides his parties, Mayslack also sponsors an annual bus trip to Chicago for a Vikings' football game, where it's always anybody's guess as to how many people actually make it to the game. He also offers free champagne with Tuesday lunches in August. "We're already getting calls for the champagne lunches," Mrs. Mayslack said.

The Mayslacks have had several offers to franchise their operations and bring Mayslack Polka Lounges into the nation's neighborhoods, but so far they've turned down the invitations.

With Mayslack now 62 years old and his wife not too many years behind, neither is overeager to start expanding the business.

"Besides, I couldn't be in two places at once to serve the sandwich," Mayslack said.

"And," his wife added, "nobody else knows how to do it."

*Logan Park Band concert about 1920s.*

# Voice of Memory Recalled of Logan Park

Too often our voices are silenced, and so our memories which are treasured, are not spoken, and not shared with others. But my memories of Logan Park, no longer have to be hidden and out of reach. Memories are meant to be shared, touched, looked at. I hope to bring to others the joy of remembering Logan Park as it was.

My memories of Logan Park go back to the '30s and the early '40s. A different time, a wonderful place to grow, play, be part of the crowd, or just a place to be. We were the generation that may not have had a lot of material things, but we were rich in being able to grow up in a time, when the parks were our way of life. In the summer, from early morning to the evening hours, Logan Park was the hub of activity. Logan had much to offer, it was our community center, a gathering of people from all walks of life, the new immigrants who came to Northeast to begin a new life, bringing with them their hopes and dreams of a better life. This community was rich with people sharing their common concerns, a place (oh, if only the grounds could talk) that was safe. A place rich with wisdom and knowledge, sharing with all...

We came to think of Logan Park as our second home. Here is where we went to meet our friends, to enjoy the many activities that were being offered to the community. Playing...sharing...growing...rich in dreams.

As a little girl, I remember sleeping in the park at night, when it got so hot and humid, with no breeze blowing, no air conditioning, but Logan Park was there to give us the shade of the cool grass to lay our blankets, giving us the opportunity to look up at the stars and know that we were safe. There was no fear of being in the park late at night, for the Park was here, for all to enjoy, the young, the old, families.

I remember the band concerts that were part of our community, giving us a chance to be part of the group. Oh, how we would sing at those band concerts on those hot nights. We would sing all the old songs. "Let Me Call You Sweetheart" or "Roll Out the Barrel," and so many more. We could bring our wagons, our blankets...put on our best clothes, because who knew who we would meet? There were the "Candy Wagons" selling all kinds of goodies, ranging from a penny to a nickel. My favorites were the Mary Jane Candy, hard taffy & peanut butter, wrapped in the yellow, black and red wrappers, and what a treat to be able to get an All-Day Sucker, Holloway, for only a nickel. (Lasted for hours, honest!!). Or, if we were extra good, we were able to get a Cheerio Ice Cream Bar on a stick. And if we were really lucky, our Cheerio Ice Cream Bar had Free printed on it, so we could get another.

Logan Park is where we went after school, perhaps to watch the boys play softball. The teams were named the Skins and the Shirts. The Skins were the ones who did not have the money to buy a shirt, but who cared? They still had fun.

The park was there for all of us to enjoy. Because no organized leagues took or used our play space, it was a park for everyone. We knew that if we broke the rules or caused trouble, Van, our Park Policeman, would bring us home. The threat of not being able to go to the park for even a few days, as that would be our punishment, was more than we would bear. We knew what our limits were and the rule was "fair play or no play." Every night we would say: "See you tomorrow, at Logan park."

By Mary Jane (Muskala) Partyka / A very quiet lady

## Logan Park History
## . . . From the Staff's Viewpoint

I became a playground instructor in 1915. In 1917, Logan became the first year-round recreation center in Minneapolis. Our athletic programs served boys, girls, men, and women. The programs included basketball, hockey, softball, football, swimming in the pool, tennis and skiing. We practiced skiing techniques in the gymnasium, then walked to Columbia Park for actual skiing.

Our gymnasium wasn't really built as a gym, but we made use of it that way. It had a baby grand piano and folding chairs, and was basically a meeting room.

The room next to the "gym" was the Logan Branch of the Minneapolis Public Library. We enjoyed using that room for our storytelling classes. There were also three club rooms and an office down the hall.

Our crafts class included activities for all ages—basket making, weaving, ceramics, and china painting, an art that is returning to popularity. Thousands of people from throughout the city came to our craft institutes.

Our dancing classes included ballet and social dancing. We rented out the gym for community dances for $5 a night.

*Dorothty Davis teaching dance class.*

Dramatics was also a popular activity. The building had no stage, so we used what was then East High School, and later Edison High School. About 300 children took part in each series of lessons.

In 1921, boy's activities began full swing with the formation of the Athletic Association. Many of our Logan boys went on to become stars at Edison High School and the University of Minnesota.

In 1929, we borrowed the Easter egg hunt idea and began an annual program that included the inevitable doll buggy parade and gave the children a chance to dress up in funny costumes and hats.

The Ice Follies came to Logan in those years as the citywide organization presented its programs at our park. Later, the Ice Follies became a national group. At Logan, it was performed on the hockey rink.

I left Logan in 1928 and came to Park Board's main office in the Courthouse as director of playgrounds

*Logan Park Ice Pageant 1925.*

and citywide pageants. I retired in 1957 after 40 years of service.

Any successes at Logan must be attributed to the support of those darling parents and of the whole community.

*Information from Alice Deitz,*
*Logan Supervisor from 1915 to 1928.*

## History of Logan Park

Logan Park has many "firsts" in the history of Minneapolis parks. It was acquired in 1883, the first year of existence of the Board of Park Commissioners. Its name was First Ward Park, later Washburn Park, and became Logan Park in 1893. The name honored John A. Logan, a general and senator from Minnesota.

Logan was the first park to adopt an active recreational program after World War I. It quickly became one of the most heavily-used parks in the city. Athletics have long been important to the Logan community, as evidenced by the many trophies won by Logan teams through the years. Logan was also among the first parks to have playground equipment, skating and hockey rinks, a toboggan slide, and an annual ice carnival. The Logan community pioneered the popular community sings of the 1920s and won citywide contests based on attendance and enthusiasm. The sings each drew thousands of people to the park.

The old Logan Building, erected in 1912, became the first site to operate year-round with recreational staff. The new community recreation center promises to provide even broader recreational experiences for future generations in the Logan community.

## Memories of Logan Park Community Center

As a child, I grew up in Logan Park. I took tap dancing lessons from Mrs. Deets. The park building at that time was a large one that housed a library, which we used faithfully. There were also classes for tiny tots to adults. On the large veranda, the band concerts were held and hundreds of people attended. Popcorn wagons lined the streets around the park. I was given a nickel to spend at each concert. This money was used to buy a Holloway sucker, which lasted for a week, by measuring how far down to eat each day.

My winter memories were at the skating rink. I rarely missed a night and we always felt safe with our friend, Mr. Van Ruden, the park police. There was also a warming house within the building, and this was a real gathering place for our friends. My memories surrounded Logan Park and are very precious to me.

*Doris Burke, 1139 Adams Street, Minneapolis, MN 55413*

I used to ice skate a lot at Logan Park from 1943–1946. We had a lot of fun. My mom had just bought me a pair of penny loafers and I wore them to the park. While I was skating, they disappeared from the warming house. I found out when I was ready to go home, I stayed till everyone left, but they didn't turn up. So I walked home in my speeder skates. It was about three blocks to home. Sure was glad when I finally got home. They weren't the easiest things to walk in.    *No name*

The park bustled with activity in the summer. There were crafts and games outside, softball, a swimming pool for children. Evenings, twenty or more families would bring picnics to the park. There was no air-conditioning, so we all went to the park. It was not unusual to see 200 to 300 people attend the band concerts. They would pass out the lyrics to all the music being done, and everyone sang along. Ice cream and lemonade was [*sic*] available for five cents.

Winter was fun, too. The entire lower level of the building was a giant warming house. There were literally hundreds [of people] on the ice every night.

Inside the building we could take piano lessons for 50 cents a lesson. There was basketball in the gym, and once a week tap dancing lessons [were] free to everyone. Dances for the neighborhood youth were held frequently in the gym also.

Enjoying all the park activities during the years I am writing about—1937 to 1942—was basically the only entertainment for most of the neighborhood. We were just coming out of the Depression, and money was scarce. The park was really a focal point of community activity.

It's nice to remember a more quiet, gentle way of life.

*Donna Gomp, 3443 Tyler St. NE Minneapolis, MN*

*Children blowing bubbles at Logan Park 1920s.*

## Logan Park Memories

I lived for almost 20 years, from 1930 to 1949, just a block and a half from Logan Park on Sixth and Jefferson Street. My two sisters, one brother and I spent many happy hours of our childhood at Logan. With four of us, I'm sure my mother encouraged us to go to the park so that she would get a little relief.

My first recollection was of walking from Webster School to the library on the east side of the old building. The books I read there whetted my appetite, and I have been an avid book reader even to this day. I also attended story hour, elocution lessons and went to craft classes in the summer months.

Of course, we enjoyed the playground and I was especially sad when the ringers were removed. I think someone had been hurt on them. We enjoyed the big slide and a small one, the swings and the sandbox. What fun we had! There was a wading pool but we were not allowed to go in it. My mother did not believe it was clean even though we saw running water. She felt some of the little ones used it as a bathroom. These were years in the '30s when we had a polio epidemic and had to be careful.

My mother would often send us to the park with a picnic lunch. We never worried about anyone molesting us. We felt safe. The presence of Officer Van contributed to our safety. He was everyone's friend. One of the treats of Logan was the pump where we could get cold water. People came with bottles to fill and take home. I don't know if it was better water than that at home, but it was nice and cold.

One of my summer memories was borrowing someone's bike and trying to learn to balance on it. I almost knocked a lady down on the sidewalk at Logan. One of our biggest events in the summer were the band con-certs. We would try to get there very early and get one of the front benches and save room for the rest of the family. It was such a fun time to sing old songs together with Harry Anderson. In our teens, we would get up about five [friends] to get a court to play tennis. In later teens, it was a good place to go in the evenings with current boyfriends.

In the winter, we spent most evenings at the skating rink. There were many times we would lose our check for the shoes and would have to walk home on our skates to get the required amount to get our shoes back. We went to the warming house in the basement of the old building. We wore woolen mittens, snow suits and hats and when they got warm and wet, it smelled awful. We had to walk through the second room to get to the boards on the sidewalk to the rink. A good night was when many boys asked us to skate. On New Years Day, we had a skating party at our church, Elim Baptist. That was an eventful day as Ed Elston, the Minneapolis Court House barber would skate with us. Actually he was strong and held us up.

I am grateful that I grew up near Logan and for the memories we have of events there. I'm sure it made the Depression years much better.

*Mrs. Doris M. (Johnson) Peterson*
*11857 Norway St. NW, Coon Rapids, MN 55448*

# Skating Pleasures of Early Days

**By Frank O'Brien**

From *Pioneer Sketches*: 1904

One cannot help contrasting the advantages people have nowadays with those when we pioneers were young. Of late years, we have had Loring Park, Powderhorn Park, and a number of the other parks kept clean from snow, with warming sheds to add to the comfort of the skaters, electric lights, and electric cars to take us to our several homes; and not only these comforts, but the satisfaction of having our skates sharpened by electricity. It is folly to waste time narrating what we have at the present day—we know it full well—but incidents of the past may prove interesting.

It is of the away-back days of our toddling city, in fact of the days when she was a mere infant, that I will tell you, when, and where we skated, and who were the skaters.

There was one winter in particular that was overflowing with enjoyment—the winter of 1860–61. It seems to me that the winters in those early times were of much longer duration than now; when they came there was no fooling, but they attended strictly to business, so that lumbermen and skaters alike knew what to depend upon.

The favorite place for skating was on the river, from the suspension bridge, now the steel arch bridge, up the river and around Nicollet Island to the East Side channel. When the snow would cover up the skating grounds, a committee made up from the boys of St. Anthony would set to work and have it shoveled off, thus giving us a pleasure resort unequaled in the western country.

The skates we used to wear were what were called "turnovers" and "stub-toes," grooved runners, with the heel corks, and straps that were secured so tightly upon the feet that circulation of the blood in those parts was next to impossible; then again, those who were obliged to wear the "stub-toe" skates, not being able to purchase the more expensive "turn-overs" with a brass knob, substituted tarred rope, such as is used to bind laths in bundles, to fasten the skates upon the feet, and, as the rope stretched, they were forced to insert "cord-wood," as it was termed, to make them fast.

If it was a very cold night or afternoon, the girls would be obliged to pull on woolen socks over their skating shoes to keep their feet from freezing while on the way from their homes to the skating grounds, and the boys would put on an extra pair of woolen socks, and pull over them well "tallered" long-legged boots, thus defying the icy sting of a long-lived winter. You may wonder why we did not wear arctics; bless your souls, such an invention had not yet reached us—the only alternative was for men and boys to put on extra socks, and the women and girls to pull [socks] over their shoes. The socks referred to were not the kind that are sold on the bargain counter of the present day, but

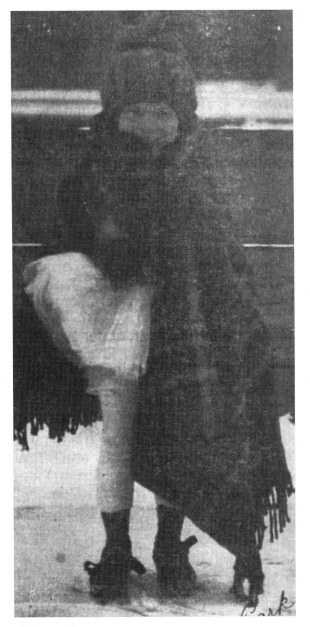

*Skating Pleasures.*

the genuine, all-wool that had been knit in the chimney corners of our old New England homes.

The greatest fun on the ice was in the evening, when a huge bonfire was made, that sent a glow of warmth to a great distance, furnished illumination for the vast piece of glassy surface, and enveloped the entire surroundings in clouds of smoke.

"Where," you may inquire, "did you obtain the inflammable material for these huge bonfires?" This information we do not feel like imparting; but we do know several parties who gave light on the subject then, and possibly they may be induced to do so now. Colonel J.H. Stevens might have had something to say about the wood pile on the bank of the river near his residence; Anthony Kelly and O.M. Laraway possibly might have alluded to boxes and sugar hogsheads; T.K. Gray, (Greely & Gray) the druggists, might tell you how he mourned the loss of rosin, tar, alcohol, and turpentine barrels; Captain Tapper possibly would tell you that portions of the island fence occasionally did their share towards contributing to the comfort and pleasure. If they cannot, who can tell?

Quite frequently during the winter we would have the brass band on the ice to discourse music for the many beautiful waltzes, the memory of which from this distance of time, is refreshing, indeed.

Some of the skaters who were expert in cutting "pigeon wings," "monograms," "backward circles," "scrolls," etc., are still in the city, fathers, mothers, grandfathers and grandmothers. In the language of the down-east Yankee: "With all your jim-crack notions nowadays, you don't begin ter have the fun we uster have!"

*Anna with her family, Anna is 4 years old and her sister Clara is 2.*

# 6  Those Were the Days

## From the Old Country
## With a Featherbed and Two Pillows

*Anna Biennias Interview*

On my first visit to the home of Anna and Matt Biennias, I noticed a bright wooden sign with the word "Vitami." The word means "welcome" in Polish, Anna informed me. A tiny white poodle named Alex follows Anna's every movement. Anna Biennias lived in Northeast Minneapolis for thirty-five years. Her husband Matt grew up on Fifteenth Avenue and Third Street in the same neighborhood as Anna. A petite woman with soft, white hair arranged in an elegant bun, Anna keeps family pictures throughout her house. Photos celebrating special events decorate the walls, while drawers hold pictures of other precious memories. Anna eagerly answers questions about her life in Northeast Minneapolis.

"I remember it all, I never forget anything," she began.

"I came from the village of Perecin, Czechoslovakia. My father was from Ujsoly, which is in the mountains in southern Poland, almost on the Czech border. My mother, my sister Clara, and I came across the ocean to America in 1908. I was two and a half years old, and Clara was only a baby.

"We rode by horse and wagon to the train station, which was a great distance from our village. Then, we took the train to Bremen, Germany. We were served a box lunch. Many of the people had never seen bananas before and bit into them without taking off the peeling. They threw the bananas out the train windows, because they tasted so bad. People that were given a piece of gum, spit it out right away because they weren't used to it.

"My father had sent money to book passage for us on the ship *Pectoria*. During our three-week trip, there was a dangerous storm on Easter Sunday. We were lucky that none of our family got seasick, but many of the other passengers were very sick. My mother was nursing Clara. Sometimes, she would nurse other babies whose mothers had taken ill. The foods we ate on the ship were eggs, meat, fresh fruit, and milk. The food and dishes on the tables would sometimes go flying from one end of the room to the other as the ship rocked during the high winds.

"There were three decks on the ship. The bottom deck was terrible because there was no air, and the people had to sleep on the dirty floor with rats and cockroaches. We were on the second floor, which wasn't so bad. The only things we brought with us from the old country were a perzina—a featherbed—and two pillows.

"When we reached Ellis Island, we spent the night in a hotel. When my mother looked out the hotel window for the first time, she thought she would see the streets paved in gold. Instead, she saw dirty streets littered with garbage.

"My mother was supposed to pick up money at the hotel, but there was no money for us. She was so scared. She knew only Hungarian and couldn't read or write. All she had was a piece of paper with an address in Minneapolis, a nine-month-old baby, a two-year-old child, and a perzina.

"Meanwhile, my father went to the Milwaukee Railroad Station in Minneapolis for three days and waited. Each day he grew more worried. Finally, he sent a telegram inquiring about us and then we received our money and were on our way.

"When we reached Minneapolis, a man put us on the streetcar that ran on Second Street, and my mother showed the conductor the piece of paper. He told her when to get off and to keep walking straight. We would meet up with someone that would give us directions, he said.

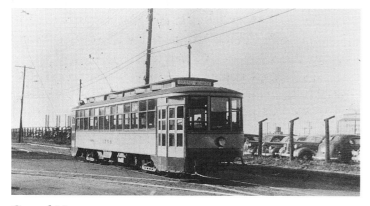

*Grand Monroe streetcar.*

"Meanwhile, my father had taken the Grand Monroe streetcar line on his way back from the Milwaukee station. We were walking up the railroad tracks going one way, and my father was coming the other way when he first saw us. His friend said, 'Look at the lady with her children.'

*Catching logs on the Bohemian Flats on the west side of the Mississippi River. One woman removes the bark with an axe.*

"That must be my wife," my father said. When my mother saw my father, she threw the bags and the baby down and almost fainted with exhaustion.

"We lived on Sixteenth and Marshall Street when I was growing up. I remember the Grain Belt sign flashing from the brewery on the river. And I remember catching the logs that floated down the river, too. A group of kids would gather, and each person would take a turn diving for a floating log. Then, we divided up the wood among each family. There was always that sharing among the people.

"My father was the delivery man for the East Side Bakery that later became Blackey's Bakery. I remember going with him on his deliveries back in the days of the horse and wagon. He delivered to the Bohemian Flats on the river. The people there were very poor and often paid him with whatever they had. My mother got really mad when he came home with chickens or ducks stuffed in his jacket instead of money.

"My father liked the Bohemian gypsies and, on Sundays, my family would go and visit them. They were friendly people that loved music and dancing. I remember an old man who wore a colorful outfit with bells on his head. He played the concertina so loud that the wallpaper peeled right off the wall.

"Our family was poor, but we always seemed to make do. We bought our shoes at the Salvation Army. When we peeled potatoes, we ate the peelings for lunch and the potatoes for supper. Sometimes, my mother took on jobs to help out. She would work at Donaldson's lunch counter and other restaurants in the downtown area.

"I worked on a truck farm that was somewhere out in the Brooklyn Park area. The truck would pick up all the kids from the neighborhood and drop them off at the farm. We worked in the hot sun, sometimes long hours, picking vegetables and weeding. We were paid ten or fifteen cents a row. They were pretty long rows. At the end of the day, the truck was never around. So, we'd have to walk all the way home. Many times we spent all our money on candy on the way home.

"I attended Holy Cross School until the eighth grade. When I went to kindergarten I didn't know English. So, the kids would laugh and call me a greenhorn. When we had lived in Czechoslovakia, we spoke Hungarian because of the Austrian-Hungarian government. But when we came to America my father insisted that I learn English, and we said our prayers in Polish. It was hard to keep the three languages straight.

"One time when I was about six years old, my mother sent me to buy milk. I had to cross Marshall Street to get to the store. In those days, the milk came in quart bottles. So, I was carrying a glass bottle. Kids were calling me names. I took that bottle and slung it across the street, and it broke in a million pieces. My mother was really mad because she had to give me two cents for another bottle."

After Anna and Matt were married, they ran a restaurant named "Ann's Grill" in Crystal. They've also owned a liquor store, a variety store, and Matt even owned a bank at one time. Anna had heard so much about Poland from her father that when she visited in 1972, the country and people all seemed very familiar. According to her father's memories, Ann didn't think that much change had occurred in Poland over the decades since he had left.

Like so many early immigrants to Northeast Minneapolis, Anna and Matt were hard-working and loved people. And when I left their house, they offered me a Polish blessing, "Ya stanzas Bogum," which means "Go with God."

# Oh, How We Sang the Polish Songs

*Connie Szczech Interview*

*Connie and friend Gladys Nesser (Case) on Easter Sunday 1937.*

After fifty-two years of waiting tables, Connie Szczech now enjoys working at Blackey's Bakery. She has lived her whole life in Northeast Minneapolis in the old section of lower Northeast surrounding Webster School. As one of six children, she grew up on Third Avenue and Madison Street. When she married at seventeen, she and her husband lived on Main Street. Connie's mother was from Medynia, a small village near Lancut in southeastern Poland and Skopania, near Rzeszow, Poland was her father's birthplace. She has visited her mother's village twice and met most of her cousins, aunts, and uncles. Her parents met and married in Minneapolis. Connie's memories of the businesses of Northeast are especially clear, probably because forty-one businesses were located within a small radius of her home during her childhood.

"In the early thirties, Northeast was a very safe place to live. We never locked the doors and were free to come and go as we pleased. Because we lived near the railroad tracks, many transients came to our door. They were welcomed and fed. They told us of the places they had been, and we enjoyed listening to them. Oh, how interesting they were!

"Mostly Polish people lived in the neighborhood, but there were also Syrians, Italians, and a few Irish families. One of our neighbors had an orchestra, and the members would practice outside. When they practiced, we danced in the streets or on the sidewalk. Whenever I hear 'Oh, Clementine,' I still think of the fun we had dancing in the street to that song.

"It was a must to go to church on Sunday for nine o'clock Mass. After Mass, friends would drop by the house. My dad played the organ, a huge old-fashioned one. Friends would bring their violins and sitars. Oh, how we sang the old Polish songs! We always had a chicken dinner on Sunday, with all the family dining together. After dinner, we would treat ourselves to a nickel double dipped ice cream cone at the corner store. Our allowance for the week was five cents.

"During the depression, my dad was out of work for two years. My mother took in boarders to make ends meet. B. F. Nelson and Kulberg Manufacturing factories were salvation for the people of Northeast Minneapolis. B. F. Nelson was a roofing and paper

*Kullberg Mfg. 610 NE Main 1925.*

manufacturing company, and Kulberg was a small cabinetmaker and lumber company. The smell of B. F. Nelson was a scent that didn't bother any of us. It smelled like tar. In fact, we enjoyed it because it meant food on our table.

"There were many small stores in our neighborhood. J. B. Hansen's was our supermarket. Groceries were always charged, and the bill paid at the end of the month. The odd amounts under fifty cents were taken off the bill. Also, a small token of appreciation was given to the customer like cookies, candies, or apples.

"Furniture had to be paid in cash when it was purchased. Now, it's the opposite. You pay cash for groceries and charge everything else.

"Sherry's Grocery was like the Byerly's of today. I still remember the water fountain sprinkling on the vegetables and fruit to keep them fresh.

"Nesser's grocery store on Third Avenue and Madison Street had the best Brownie Root Beer. The Brownie Beverage Company was in the middle of the block on Third Avenue. Later, Brownie sold out to Seven Up. Dad's Root Beer is the closest to the taste of Brownie Root Beer.

"Once a week my dad would bake bread. It was an egg bread filled with raisins and baked in a nine by thirteen inch pan. Oh, how high it grew and how delicious it was! We didn't have a garden because we had a small yard. My aunt lived near the railroad tracks where there was a lot of land, so she had a huge garden. She supplied us with vegetables, apples, cherries, and rhubarb. Whenever we visited my aunt, she always served us Jello, which was a special treat at that time.

"We spent summer vacations at Como Park and Lake Nokomis. My father had an old truck. He put a couple of boards on the back, so we would have a place to sit. Then, he would drive all six of us, plus all the neighborhood kids to Lake McCarron in St. Paul. As we were going up hill on County Road B, the boys had to get out of the truck and help push. We would go every day. Our lunch was always the same, hardboiled eggs, oranges, and apples.

"My dad enjoyed traveling. He made us read about geography and study maps. Then, we would pretend we were traveling. My mother always insisted we talk Polish at home. She said the more languages we could speak, the better for us. She did a lot of crocheting and sewing. She made all of our clothes, so we were well-dressed. She also did a lot of canning, and we

*Fidelity Bank, F.W. Woolworth and Christianson Bakery 1947.*

made our own sauerkraut. Oh, how we hated to make it! We had to jump on the sauerkraut, and the smell would stay with us for days. Other children would make fun of us.

"Movies were five cents. My favorites were the ones starring Ginger Rogers and Fred Astaire. Ken Magnan was the cowboy movie star of the day.

"Logan Park had a beautiful building. In the summer, there were band concerts, swimming, and ball games. In the winter, there was ice skating. We loved to go down to the warming house and mingle with our friends. Across from the park was Amble's Confectionery, where they made their own ice cream. It was a hangout for most of us. On Third Avenue and Fourth Street, we had an ice house. What fun it was to watch how the ice was delivered down the shaft to us! Large chunks of ice would slide from the top of the bridge down a wooden slide to the customer's wagons. The noise and the sight were fascinating. We seldom went downtown because we were close to East Hennepin. Almost anything our family needed could be found there.

"During Lent, we were not allowed to go to the movies or to eat sweets. But come Holy Saturday at noon, Lent was over. Then, we feasted on the sweets. The last week of Lent, the mirrors were covered with dish towels. I still don't know why![1]

"On Holy Thursday, we would visit churches in Northeast Minneapolis. They claim there are more churches in Northeast Minneapolis than any place else in the world. We visited All Saints, St. Constantine, St. Maron's, St. Boniface, St. Anthony, St. Cyril's, Holy Cross, St. Hedwig's, and Our Lady of Lourdes.

"On Good Friday, no radio or music was allowed to be played. From noon to three o'clock, we couldn't even talk. On Holy Saturday, we prepared an Easter basket with food. The basket was filled with Polish sausage, ham, lamb of butter,[2] horseradish, hard-boiled eggs, and homemade bread. We would take the basket to church and have it blessed. Also ground, pickled beets with horseradish were also blessed. This was delicious!

"On Easter Sunday after church, we would have a big breakfast. It consisted of an Easter barszcz. Even today, an Easter Sunday doesn't go by without our Easter barszcz. We always had a new Easter outfit complete with hat, gloves, and patent leather shoes. How we loved to show off!

"Advent wasn't observed as faithfully as Lent but come Christmas Eve, no meat was served. A feast of thirteen different foods was served as soon as the first star appeared in the sky. And we always had an empty seat at the table for an unexpected guest. After dinner, we sang Christmas carols until it was time to go to midnight Mass. On Christmas Day, a huge dinner was served. The day after Christmas, we visited friends and relatives. We threw nuts as we entered their homes. It was to remind us of St. Stephen being stoned to death.

"The thought of Polish weddings brings happy memories. Most of them were held at P. N. A. Hall[3] on

--------

1. Looking in the mirror was considered vain. All signs of vanity were to be avoided during Lent.

2. Butter shaped into a lamb by a gelatin mold or double-sided cake mold. This symbol served as a representation of Jesus as a sacrificial lamb.

3. This abbreviation refers to the Polish National Alliance.

Thirteenth Avenue and Fourth Street or the O. D. H. S. Hall on Fifteenth Avenue and Second Street. The smaller weddings were held at P. W. E. Hall[4] on Thirteenth Avenue and Second Street. Mrs. Laviski was the cook for weddings, later on, Mrs. Jaworski and Mrs. Hazzy. I remember this because I often helped the caterers serve the food.

"Whole families were invited to every wedding. The couple went to the guest's homes and invited them personally. The guests would arrive about four o'clock for the reception and were greeted at the door by an accordion or concertina player. The same song was played over and over again, and the guests would drop change in the concertina. Dinner was served about five o'clock, and music followed. How we danced! That's how children learned to dance—going to Polish weddings.

"After a couple hours of dancing, they had the bridal dance. Chairs were put in a semicircle, and each guest would dance with the bride. The guest would throw a coin at a plate and try to break it. At that time, silver dollars were plentiful. If the plate was broken, it meant good luck for the couple. That dance lasted an hour. Then, the groom would enter the circle, dance once around the circle, and carry his bride off the floor. The bride would take off her veil and put it on her maid of honor. This meant the maid of honor was the hostess for the rest of the evening."

Connie feels the neighborhood has changed a great deal. All but seven of the original homes of her youth have been torn down and replaced by condos or new homes. Children no longer run free, and people don't watch out for one another in the same way. But Connie continues to pass on the old traditions to the younger members of her family. Together, they still break the Oplatek wafer at Christmas and bring food baskets to church for the Easter blessing.

### How to Make Sour Kraut

Wash and Core Cabbage.
Shred it on a large shredder into a large crock.
Add a little salt and more cabbage until crock is full.
Stamp cabbage down, add more salt and cabbage if needed.
   (Small children could fit into crock)
Cover the cabbage with a wooden cover to fit crock.
Place a huge rock on top of wooden cover to weigh
   the cabbage down. Place a clean towel over that.

### Bialy Barszcz Wielkanocna
### (White Easter Barszcz)

2 lbs. Polish butcher shop smoked kielbasa
Approx. 10 cups of cold water
4 tbsp. white vinegar
4–5 tbsp. flour made into paste
4 eggs, slightly whisked
½ pint light sweet cream
salt & pepper, to taste

In a large pot, bring kielbasa to a boil. Reduce heat and simmer for 20–25 minutes. Turn off heat and let meat rest in water for 20 minutes. Remove meat and reheat stock. Add vinegar and flour made into a paste with 6 tbsp. or more cold water. Stir into stock until slightly thickened. Whisk eggs and sweet cream into a qt. size bowl. Ladle hot stock into egg mixture and then into stock, stirring constantly to prevent curdling.

   Serve with potatoes, ham, kielbasa and hard-boiled eggs.

---

4. This abbreviation refers to an association named Polish White Eagles.

## Papa Worked in a Polish Whiskey Factory

### Jean Kobus Interview

Jean Kobus lives on Tyler Street in a stucco house with her two cats. Furnished with some pieces of modern furniture and a few touches of the old-world style Jean's house is as comfortable as her manner. A back hall and bathroom updated the original structure and the ancient furnace was converted from a coal stove. But ceramic doorknobs and metal, push-button light switches evoke the standard construction features of 1904 Northeast Minneapolis. Jean lived in Northeast almost all of her life, except for the five years her father owned a barbershop in the nearby Seven Corners area of Minneapolis.

"I remember when there used to be a lake where Columbia Park is now. There were horse races around the lake, and people came from all around to watch them. I remember, too, when Bottineau Park did not exist. A row of buildings about two blocks long with apartments of about twenty units each was on that land.

"Papa was from Gdansk, which is on the northern tip of Poland. He worked in a whiskey factory that was run by the Polish government. Mama was born and raised in Warsaw. They met and were married in Warsaw in 1907. Papa came to America in 1909. His in-laws gave him money to go to a barber school and establish himself in America. He went to Poland twice to try and convince Mama to join him, but she was happy in Poland and did not wish to come here.

Finally, Mama came over in 1912 with my older sister, who was about five years old at the time. The trip

*Jean's Parents, Adam and Julia Samoker on their wedding day in Warsaw, Poland 1905.*

across the ocean took three to six weeks. They stayed in a small room on the ship. It was not as good as first class, but much better than steerage. The waters were rough, and both mama and my sister were sick. The ship first stopped at Newfoundland and then came down the coast to land at Ellis Island. By train, my mother and sister made their way to Minneapolis.

"Papa had been renting a small house in North Minneapolis on Lowry and Second Street. He had only a stove, a table with four chairs, a bed, and a nightstand.

After taking a nine-month course at Molar Barber College, Papa opened a small barbershop near Sokul's Bar on Twenty-second and University Avenue Northeast. He walked to work each day across the Lowry Bridge. Mama was not happy about living in this small room. She was also very lonesome for her parents.

"We joined the Sacred Heart National Church on Twenty-second Avenue. Our church was different than the other churches in the area. Although it was Catholic, it was not governed by the Pope, and there were no nuns. The church for our family was the center of our social life. Every Sunday night, there would be a dance that children and parents would attend. A Polish band would play, and everybody would dance. I loved these dances. On Saturday mornings, we went to Polish school, which was also at the church. Here we learned both the Polish language and Polish history. The church was the hub of our life.

"In 1921, when I was five years old, our family moved to 514 Twenty-second Avenue Northeast to be closer to Papa's barbershop and our church. We were within two blocks of each. In those days, it was very important to live near the church. Our house was a brick duplex with a chicken coop in the backyard.

"At first, we had gaslights that had a wick in the center and two chains. My father thought they were dangerous and didn't give off enough light. So, he had electricity installed. We had a big, round stove in the living room that was fueled by coal. The stove was covered with Isinglass[5] windows. There was also a railing that surrounded the stove, that kept us from getting burned. We always put our feet on the railing to warm up.

"Because we only had an icebox, we went to the store every day. Every block had a grocery store, some had two or three. We didn't have a garden, so we bought all our vegetables at the store. We kept the potatoes and carrots in the basement in a sand pit.[6] We bought the vegetables in the fall and buried them. Mama would say, 'Go down the basement and get carrots.' I hated doing that because I would get sand in my fingernails.

"My father would not eat canned vegetables, so we had to keep a large supply. In the summer, we bought our fresh vegetables at the Farmer's Market stands at Lake Minnetonka. He also would not allow us to use soap for washing dishes. He said it was made out of horse's hooves. So, we had to take extra time using very hot water for washing and scalding the rinse water. I remember washing the kitchen floor on my hands and knees, then spreading newspaper on the floor.

"My mother never made bread. We bought Polish rye at Blackey's Bakery on the way home from church. The white bread, we bought at the grocery store. We always had to eat the old bread first. It was not till I was older that I realized we were eating old bread all the time.

"Rendering lard was something that had to be done every few months. We bought a big hunk of leaf lard at the butcher shop. It was called that because it was shaped like a leaf. The lard was divided into five containers. Then, we melted it on the stove and strained it into large pottery jugs. I remember the smell of

_____
5. A primitive glass resembling crystallized ice commonly used from the 1910s through the 1930s. Often produced in Russia, these panes provided excellent thermal insulation and were used in lanterns, coal-burning stoves, and even automobile windows.

_____
6. Sand helped extend the life of fresh vegetables in days without modern refrigeration.

*Holland school 1707 NE Washington St. 1905.*

grease would permeate the house. We would use this lard all winter for frying. After rendering lard, we had a special treat. The leftover pieces of crispy, fried fat were crumbled and made into cookies. It was the only time we ever had cookies. The lard was stored in the basement in the root cellar.

"We always had roast on Sundays. It would be cooking in the oven while we were at church. We had cakes on Sunday, too. The next day, we would have pierogi made with the ground up roast beef and a little gravy. Pierogis can also be stuffed with potatoes or cheese, but we never ate them that way.

"One of my favorite foods, which I still love today, is called chlodnik. It's a combination of pig's feet and pig's hocks boiled with a little water. After the pork cools, you take the meat off the bones and place it in a bread pan. It makes a gelatin like headcheese.

"One of our regular, mainstay meals was chicken soup. Mama used a stewing hen, not a fryer, which we bought at Johnson's Ready Meats. When I was little, I was sent to the store and I would tell the meat man, 'We want the feet.' Mama scalded and skinned the feet, then added this to the soup. We didn't eat the feet, of course, but they were used to bring out the juices and add flavor to the soup. Mama would point to the soup and say 'Look oitchuh,' which meant 'chicken eyes are looking at you.' Actually, it was the fat on top of the soup.

"Easter was a very special holiday at our house. Christmas and Easter were both important, but Easter had a more religious connotation. We always baked ham with cloves, which made the house smell nice. We also had bapka, a bread made with egg yolks and yeast that is baked in a three-pound coffee can. After baking, the bread was topped with an icing glaze that dripped down the sides and colored sugar was sprinkled on the top.

"We also had colored hard-boiled eggs, but our method of dying them was different than today. We used red onion skins that were saved for weeks. After boiling the skins and eggs together in hot water, the eggs turned a rusty, orange color. Each egg was the same color.

"In 1925, the normal dress for a young girl of school age like me included beige stockings on top of long underwear. The stockings were held up with round elastic garters. Black bloomers came down to my knees. On top of them, I wore a skirt and sweater or blouse made of cotton in the summer and wool in the winter. On Sundays, I wore white stockings instead of beige.

"My hair was worn in a Dutch boy hairdo that was always neat and trim, because my father was a barber. During the week, I wore black tie oxford shoes. I would keep wearing my oxfords, even when they were badly torn. If I were going shopping for shoes, I didn't want my mother to go with me. She would make me buy the practical oxfords, while my father would let me buy Mary Janes. I loved my black patent leather Mary Janes that were only for Sundays. There was a strap and a button across the front. The night before church, I'd rub Vaseline on my Mary Janes to keep the leather shiny and pliable.

"I went to Holland School until about the fourth grade. I remember the fire drills where all the students on the second floor slid down a metal chute that was on the outside of the building. We moved to Seven Corners when my father expanded his barbershop, and I continued my education at Clay and Jackson School in Southeast. Later, we moved back to Northeast Minneapolis, and I went to Edison High. The day after graduation day, our senior class went on a picnic to Taylors Falls. Today's seniors still go there.

"During high school, I worked at Powers Department Store in downtown Minneapolis selling hosiery. I made twenty-five cents an hour. Stores were not open in the evenings or on Sundays, so I worked only on Saturdays. My first job after high school was at the Farmers Insurance Company downtown. It was difficult getting a job in the '30s, there were never any jobs in the paper. I got the job through an employment agency. I overheard a man at the agency giving an address to the girl in front of me. I went to that address and said the agency sent me, and I got the job."

Jean worked for the Board of Education for twenty-four years as a secretary and is now retired. She continues to take classes whenever possible through a program called Elder Hostel and often stays in dorms with the younger students at various colleges. The neighborhood of Jean's youth has changed little in the last eighty years. She says the streets have the same neat, single homes with trimmed hedges and fenced-in yards that remind her of special childhood experiences and friends.

## Life in Italy Was Very Hard

*Sam Mancino Interview*

Sam spent his early life in the Northeast area, first on Buchanan Street, then later on Pierce and Summer Streets. Now retired from the post office after thirty-two years of service, he speaks fondly of Northeast and remembers the good life in this community.

"My father came to New York from Italy in 1919. A people broker[7] put him on a train and shipped him off in a boxcar to Utah. He had no idea where he was going. He only knew there was a job waiting for him in the coal mines.

"My father made about $20 a week in the mines and saved enough to take a train to Clarksburgh, West Virginia. He joined his fellow countrymen and family working in the coal mines. Six years later, he was able to raise enough money to return to Italy to bring over my mother and older brother. My parents were from San Giovanni in Fiore, a province which is in Southern Italy. Life for them in Italy was very hard. We should all be glad that they were able to come to the United States and raise their family here, they said.

"When I was twelve, my family moved to Northeast Minneapolis. Almost all the Italian families had come from Clarksburgh. Many people were from the same towns as my parents. Living in Northeast, we did not have to lock our doors or take other precautions for safety. Each family had a well-tended garden. Some gardens were in the backyards and others were along the railroad tracks.

*Sam Mancino and his wife Theo with Sam Jr. 734 Pierce St. 1949.*

"Because most of the people came from the same part of Italy, the foods cooked and eaten were much the same. Spaghetti with homemade noodles and fresh baked bread was served often.

"The most traveling we did was shopping or going to the movies. Very few people owned cars. My older brother, Russell, bought one and taught me to drive. Then I would take my parents and some neighbors shopping on the Avenue.[8]

---

7. People who recruited employees for businesses

8. East Hennepin Avenue. A main commercial district.

"The Maple Leaf grocery was run by three Canadian brothers and one sister. They were generous with credit. I remember paying the bill one time and asking Mr. Al, one of the three brothers, why he gave credit when the merchants on the Avenue were not so free. To which Mr. Al replied 'We have not lost a cent due us from the Italian people in this neighborhood.' He always was generous with candy when the bill was reduced or paid in full.

Every year the Italians celebrate July 17th, commemorating the founding of their church of Our Lady of Mount Caramel. On this feast day the men from the parish parade their statue of Our Lady down the street, which was brought over from the village of San Giovanni in Italy. They set down the statue in the yard or on the sidewalks and people pin money to the statue.

Another feast day includes January 7th—Little Christmas or LaBafana where we met in the church basement. The people from the parish played games and everyone brought a special dish to share. The older adults reminisced about the old days in Italy. But this is no longer celebrated.

"My friends and I took our dates to the theater on Saturday nights. Cheech Spano, the usher, would come down the aisle and flash his light. 'No monkey around tonight,' he'd always say. Movies cost ten or fifteen cents. On Tuesday nights, there were drawings for crockery plates. As a member of the Roy Rogers Fan Club, you could get one free Saturday movie a month and other gifts. The most popular Western actors were Red Grange and Hop-A-Long Cassidy. The comics we liked were the Three Stooges, the Marx Brothers and Crazy Cats.

*Ritz Theater
1953.*

"The movie houses were the Princess Theater on Fourth and East Hennepin and the Ritz on Thirteenth and Fourth Street. My friends and I used to stop at the Polish bakery next door to the Ritz. You could get a nice piece of poppy seed bread or a kolachy for just a nickel. My parents went to the Bijou Theater on Washington Avenue. With double feature and low budget

*Sheridan Elementary and Middle School 1201 University Ave NE 1920.*

*Pierce Elementary School 1121 NE Broadway 1920.*

films, they could spend a whole afternoon at the movies for only ten or fifteen cents.

"I went to grade school at Pierce Elementary, which was on Fillmore and Broadway. It's been gone for many years now. Then, I attended Sheridan Middle School and Edison High School. Once my friends and I were dismissed from school for hitching rides on trucks. We could not return until our parents came with us. But my parents were so busy with children and work that they could not go to school. In addition, I would have to translate which was really a bother.

We were finally readmitted even though our parents never made it to school.

"My two brothers, Joe and Russ Mancino, owned the Town Pump Bar after they came back from the war. It was located on Eighth and Marshall Street and was frequented by the Grain Belt Brewery crowd."

Sam especially remembers that the whole neighborhood took it very hard when a child died because they all knew each other so well. Neighbor women would clean house, wash diapers, and cook meals while the family went to the cemetery. In the old days, bodies were shown in the homes. And often, the funeral lasted two or three days after the burial. Families and friends would share memories of the deceased and, in that way, comfort their bereaved neighbors.

## Elsie Brunner Let Us Use Her Bathroom for Bath Time

*Pat Eaton Interview*

Pat Eaton's maternal grandfather George Mortimer was born in 1840 at Fort Snelling and later served in the Civil War. His father Richard Mortimer came to

*Her grandparent's wedding, Karl and Sophie Schjoll 1900.*

America at the age of nineteen from Leeds, England. Pat's mother was Scottish, Irish, and English. Her father was a second-generation Norwegian from the Schjoll Farm in Skria. As a writer and proud Grandma, Pat feels a need to preserve all history, but especially family history.

"As a young child, I thought Northeast Minneapolis was between Twenty-seventh Avenue and St. Anthony Boulevard from McKinley to Benjamin. I was told never to go beyond those streets. Our family moved from St. Anthony Boulevard to McKinley Street in 1937 when I was three and my sister was six months old. We lived in the garage that summer while our new house was being built and our old house had been sold. Elsie Brunner, a new neighbor of ours that lived across the alley, let us use her bathroom for our bath time. I still have warm and happy feelings when I bathe in a tub with ceramic tile on the walls and I think of Elsie's tub.

"Paul Sandell, our next door neighbor, owned the block. Dad bought a lot and a half from him. Our neighbors were all about the same age. All the men were working; all the mothers stayed home. I had twenty mothers and dads. Every neighbor would give me cookies, so I was a very chubby child.

"The neighborhood was safe. We only locked our house when we went to bed. Our screen porch had only a hook, and the French doors leading into the living room had a simple tap bolt. Our kitchen table had booths, not chairs, around it and was decorated in pink and grey, which were very popular colors in the '30s and '40s. Our door was always open, and our house was said to be the hub of the neighborhood. My mother served coffee every day except Sunday to six or eight mothers. Sunday was family and church day.

"My father never minded when the ladies came over and was always congenial. He'd go downstairs to his woodworking shop in the basement furnace room.

I often went with him when he went shopping at Wards for his supplies. He subscribed to *Popular Mechanics* and shared the magazine with all the neighbors. He built cabinets, desks, and shelves for all the bedrooms.

"We lived on the bus route. My father took the bus to work every weekday at 7:30 and came home at 5:30. Dinner was always on the table ready for the family to eat. He worked at the Northwestern Bell Telephone Building as an engineer on the twenty-second floor. My sister and I went to visit him once or twice. It was fun to look out the windows and see all the downtown area.

"The doctor, the dentist, and even the teachers were our neighbors. We took the bus to the dentist on Central Avenue. My parents bought their furniture from Billman's on Central Avenue. Our food, clothing, entertainment, church, school, friends, and relatives were all within one mile of our home. A man delivered our milk and our food. Once a month, my mother would drive to the grocery store to pay the bill. I would find the butterscotch cookie jar and take one cookie. After my mother paid the bill, she would be given a large grocery bag of fruit or vegetables.

"My grandmother worked at Johnson Sisters Department Store on Central Avenue, and we would visit her. She was a sales lady and seamstress. When customers paid for their purchases, my grandmother would put the sales slip in a canister. The canister traveled along a wire to the cash register in the back of the store and would be returned with the receipts.

"My dad bought all his suits from Eklund Clothing Store on East Hennepin whose owners were our neighbors. On the Fourth of July, we would drive to the Eklund's lake home to celebrate the day. Their home had a screened in porch that faced the lake. We never owned a cabin of our own so it was a special place.

*Eklund's Clothing Store in 1912 N.P. Eklund is standing on far right.*

"All my friends lived Northeast. Through grade school, Brownies, Girl Scouts, and high school I acquired friends. Many of them lived within six blocks of my home. Our mothers were also acquainted. Eighteen of us were inseparable, and we formed our own club. We went everywhere together and, as grandmothers, we are still together. When my parents died, my husband and I moved into the family home on McKinley. We are daughter and son to many of our original residents still living on the block. Now, my grandchildren visit Elsie Brunner who always has cookies for them.

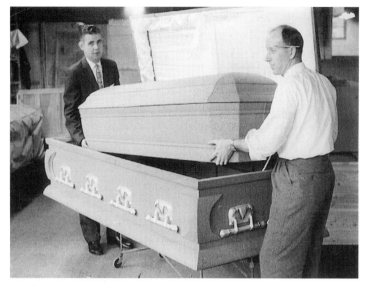

*Bob Berny.*

## It's Just the Way Things Were

*Bob Berny Interview*

Bob Berny recently retired as president and manager of the Northwest Casket Company. As a child, he lived with his family on Tenth and Marshall Street Northeast. Bob still meets six of his friends from Northeast once a month, and they all have a good time talking about the old days.

"My father worked at Will's Motors, which was right next to the Wilcox factory on Tenth and Marshall Street. The company made car heaters. Dad was watchman from 1920 until 1936. I remember carrying a hot dinner in a cardboard box, down to my father while he was working. Tropic Air and then Grayco replaced the original company.

"My family rented a house on 1001 Second Street during the Depression. The house was a mansion that dated back to the Civil War. Sixteen rooms were divided between two families. The scroll work and ornate design of the woodwork was unique. A large wooden plate rail surrounded the entire living room and dining room. Between the living room and dining room were huge doors that would slide into the wall. These rooms were probably once used as a ballroom. The house was close to 100 years old when it was torn down.

"I went to school from 1932 to 1939 at St. Anthony of Padua Grade School. All the kids worked in those days; it's just the way things were. My first job was delivering newspapers when I was eleven years old. I delivered papers in the area for two cents each. But I remember getting five cents from the patrons at the Town Pump, a local tavern on Eighth and Marshall Street.

*Workers at John F. Wilcox Sash and Door Company 1915.*

142

"We would start out early in the morning, picking up the papers at the paper shack on 1225 Second Street. We'd buy the papers for one cent each and sold them for two cents each. The Sunday paper cost six cents and sold for ten cents. The work averaged about two hours a day with a profit of nineteen cents per customer each month. Delivery during the Armistice Day storm took about four hours.

"I quit the paper route in the spring of 1941 and went to work part time at the Second Street Market on Twelfth Avenue and Second Street. In the fall of 1942, I quit there and went to work on the 3 to 11 shift at Ry-O-La at Tenth and Main Street. It was the bakery that made Ry-Krisp, and we were paid forty-five cents per hour.

"In the old days, clothes were more important than now. Parents couldn't buy clothes for their kids, so they had to work and buy their own. No one had much, but all of us kids would try to look nice, and we took good care of our clothes. For school, we'd dress up in a white shirt and a sweater or, sometimes, a suit or sportcoat. Dress shoes or penny loafers were popular.

"As for fun, I was always into sports as a teenager. We had very few organized sports, but we would start a game whenever we had a bat and a baseball or a football and a vacant lot to play in.

"I dropped out of high school in December of 1942 because I could not keep up going to school and working full time, and the money was more important than school. Times were uncertain. The country was just recovering from the Depression, so money was very important. And with the war on, it was just a matter of time before I would be in the service.

"In January of 1943, I got a day job with Northwest- ern Casket Company. I earned top wages in those days. Working for Northwestern Casket was my first daytime job. I worked for a remarkable man named Earl Thulen. He had started at the company in 1916 when he was sixteen years old, and he was the man that made the wheels go around at Northwestern Casket Company. He taught me more than any person I have ever known. I suppose I learned some work ethics as a paper boy. After all, we had to deliver a paper seven days a week and fifty-two weeks out of the year. However, I learned more about ethics, responsi- bility, and general common sense from Earl Thulen than any other source.

"I bought my first car in the spring of 1943. I paid $85 for a 1933 Chevrolet. It was hard to buy a car in those days because of the war. All metals were used in the production of jeeps, tanks, ships, and airplanes.

"In January of 1944, I joined the Navy and served two and a half years. I was discharged in June of 1946. The following year Earl Thulen asked me to come back to work for him. I did and I'm still there. I was married in September of 1953 and have three chil- dren—two girls and one boy."

Bob claims he has no hobbies. However, he does have many interests. His biggest interest is still North- western Casket Company. He is part owner and goes in to work a few days a week. Of his other interests, bowling is his favorite sport. He also plays a little golf and does some fishing. He doesn't hunt anymore, but goes along with his son and nephew and does the cooking. According to Bob, Northeast has changed a great deal over the years. Many of the duplexes are owned by absentee landlords, and neighbors don't seem to know each other any more.

# To America from the Ukraine in 1915

*Olga Pawluk Interview*

*Olga Pawluk dressed in Ukrainian costume.*

Olga Pawluk's home mirrors her love for ethnic things. A special serving dish in a traditional red and white Ukrainian design rests on a small table. Three red and white Ukrainian pillows Olga embroidered adorn the couch. Meticulously decorated eggs and other Ukrainian treasures are carefully arranged in the curio cabinet. Each year she contributes and participates in the Ukrainian exhibit in the Festival of Nations at the St. Paul Civic Center. Olga usually works in the Ukrainian kitchen making foods like Holubtsa cabbage rolls, pyrohy, and Ukrainian sausage. Easter eggs are displayed and sold at a table for the Ukrainian Gift Shop where Olga works.

"My parents came to America from the Ukraine in 1915. My father Peter Haywa was from Pidhaytsi. My mother was from Galacia[9]. They met in Detroit where he proposed. They were later married in Minneapolis.

"My father first lived in a boarding house in Hopkins. He was active in plays and choir at the church so he biked over to St. Constantines Ukrainian Church in Northeast Minneapolis several times a week as well as on Sunday. Throughout his lifetime, he worked for many places including the Soo Line Railroad. He worked the longest for Crown Iron Works as a blacksmith, and he made pontoons for the army during World War II.

"I was born February 14th, 1918 in a house on Harrison Street Northeast. Mostly Ukrainian families lived in the neighborhood from Fourth Street to Broadway and from Harrison Street to the river. My family lived in a small apartment in the house, which was right alongside the railroad tracks for several years. Later, we moved to Madison Street into the Slavic area, and then to a four-flat on Ninth and University[10]

"Because we shared our living space with four other families, we had a big backyard to play in. The

---

9. Austria-Hungarian controlled territory in southeastern Poland and northwestern Ukraine.
10. A building with four separate units.

games we played were "Run, Sheep, Run," "Annie, Annie Over" and stick ball. On Saturday afternoons we would go to the movies at the Princess Theater on East Hennepin and later, the Ritz Theater.

*Everett School 604 University Ave. NE 1936.*

"I went to many different schools because my family had to move often. School was hard at first because I spoke no English, but I learned in half a year. I went to Sheridan, Edison High, Everett, and St. Boniface. I remember that at Sheridan the teachers were very strict. In those days, teachers had the right to reprimand students with occasional slaps and paddles. The principal at Sheridan, Mr. Mooney, had a paddle in his office called the "Red Owl," which was used on naughty students.

"Our church was the center of our community. I was really active in our church, St. Michael's Ukrain-

ian Orthodox. On Sunday evenings, my family would walk to church for classes or other events. By the time we arrived at the church, a whole group of people would have joined us. The church had big events in the hall at least once a month, and each time we would decorate the hall. In addition to weekly choir rehearsals, we always had something else going on like plays and dances. Doing the plays was great fun. I acted or directed or did something in every one of them. The dances were fun except there weren't very many Ukrainian boys that participated. In high school, I'd say that about half of us girls dated Ukrainians, and the other half dated non-Ukrainians.

"Our family didn't take trips when I was growing up, but we did go to Twin Lake and Bass Lake for picnics. We played softball and had races. Men and women of all ages participated. Logan Park always had programs for the neighborhood children. The park building had a library, and we used to sit in there and read after school.

"Contact with the other ethnic groups was mostly through school and at the parks. The Polish had their own schools, but they were integrated into the rest of the school system in the 1950's.

"We did our shopping at Harasyn's grocery store, it's where Emily's Deli is now on Seventh and University. The original owners of Harasyns came from the same town as my father. Mr Harasyn and my father would always have long talks in Ukrainian. We didn't go to the bakery because my mother baked our bread—big loaves of egg bread.

"Ukrainians celebrate Christmas on January 7th. Christmas Eve supper on January 6th is very special. The table is set with an extra place for the unexpected guest, Jesus. The traditional meal consists of twelve dishes, but no meat or cheese. The head of the family takes the first spoonful then gives a wish of happiness and good health for the coming new year. Then the bowl is passed around, and each person takes one spoonful.

*Traditional Christmas Meal*

Ritual Dish—Katya (wheat cooked)
Appetizer—pickled herring and pickled mushroom
Entrees—Borscht (beet soup)
Holubtsi (cabbage rolls with rice or buckwheat)
Sauerkraut with peas
Varensky (pyrohy or piorgi with potato and sauerkraut)
Baked stuffed fish, fish aspic or fish balls
Mushrooms and gravy
Desserts—Kolach (big round decorated Christmas bread, must have X mark of Christmas, shaped into a round braid)
Medivnyk (honey cake or honey cookies)
Fruit soup
Nuts and Candy

"The next day we sing carols, but we do not exchange gifts. We do this on St. Nicholas Day, which is before Christmas. Our church choir always goes to sing to the priest on Christmas Day. Sometimes the choir will go out to homes and sing carols.

Olga has worked hard to preserve her Ukrainian heritage. Carrying on the tradition, her daughter learned to play the bandura, which has 48 strings but resembles a large guitar. At parties, local orchestras often play a medley of Ukrainian songs. This is the cue for the young Ukrainians to go to the center of the room and dance to melodies from the homeland as the older generation smiles proudly from the sidelines. This is a time of merriment, a time of honor, a time of reflection and a special tribute to the older generations.

# I Went to Our Lady of Lourdes Notre Dame School

*Evelyn Lund Interview*

Evelyn came with her grandparents to live in Northeast Minneapolis from Range, Wisconsin when she was about twelve. Her grandfather originally came from Three Rivers, Canada, and her grandmother was French. Evelyn grew up on Fillmore Street. She worked as a homemaker for vacationing parents but is now retired. Family photos in ornate frames, an extensive doll collection, and other treasures acquired in the years gone by are displayed throughout her beautifully decorated house. She dances with a Hopkins group of square dancers called the "Golden Swingers" and makes her own costumes. As a candidate for Senior Raspberry Queen of the Hopkins Raspberry Festival, Evelyn traveled around Minnesota.

"I went to Our Lady of Lourdes Notre Dame school. It was a four-room school taught by the Sisters of St. Joseph with a convent next door. Most of the kids were French, but there were a few Italian and Lebanese children. The French settlement was within a seven block radius surrounding the school, from University Avenue to Adams and from about Fourth to Eighth Avenues. There were once boarding houses on Second Street in back of the church and also in the Flats on Third and University. Most of the buildings have been torn down now. The Lebanese people lived near the Fifth Street bridge in old Flats, not far from Nesser's grocery store.

"The school choir was a very important social group for me. We went places together and were good

*Evelyn Lund and her brother Leo Carpentier in 1914.*

friends. For family outings we would take the trolley for a picnic on Sunday afternoon. We went to White Bear Lake, Excelsior Park, or Longfellow Gardens near Minnehaha Falls. We skated at Logan Park in the winter, and this was a very popular place to meet up with friends. I don't know how we could get around to do things with the long skirts and long underwear we wore. Girls didn't wear slacks back then. Also the girls wore black skates, something that is unheard of today.

"Schulo's was the neighborhood grocery store. We did our shopping on East Hennepin, which was a thriving business district back then. Often, the area was so busy you could hardly walk on the sidewalks. There was a J.C. Penneys, a Woolworth's, and a drugstore complete with a soda fountain. The Princess Theatre was a really big deal for us kids. Saturday matinees with double feature were only five cents. All of my friends would be there. Sometimes, they gave away dishes and had cooking lessons on stage. The Blue Ribbon Meat Market was owned by a Frenchman,

*Our Lady of Lourdes School 5th Street and 6th Avenue NE 1888-1959.*

Harry Gagnon, and Dr. Lapierre and his son were the doctors on East Hennepin.

"It is a French tradition to have big dinners on Sundays. For holidays, we had ground pork, split pea soup with ham, and French meat pies called tourtierre. They still sell these at Our Lady of Lourdes church for fund-raising. On Christmas Eve, we always went to Midnight Mass. We had lots of home parties where we would move the furniture and roll up the rug. We often danced to the peppy music of an accordian, dulcimer, the piano, or a fiddle. We did some square dancing and waltzes. I remember there were always babies on the bed during these parties. We often gathered at the Archambeau's house on Van Buren by the bridge. It was great fun.

"All of my uncles worked for the Great Northern Railroad on Central and Van Buren. They were engineers, trainmen, and switchmen. Lots of families from school worked at B. F. Nelson. The dirt and smell from the roofing company was terrible. I remember the dirt would collect on the porches, and we would have to clean them all the time. And we'd always smell the pickles from the Gedney pickle factory when crossing the Lowry Bridge.

"Northeast has not really changed a lot since I was younger. Some of the buildings are gone now and new businesses have come in, but Fillmore Street still looks familiar. Many of the French people from Our Lady of Lourdes church moved and started up St. Charles Borromeo church and built another community there.

"A few years back we held an all school reunion for Our Lady of Lourdes Notre Dame School. Over 300 people from all over the world attended. The reunion was held in the church basement. First, the banquet was held, then we went to Mass. In the evening, we had dinner at Jax Restaurant. My whole family attended because we all went to the school. We had great fun talking about the old days and how lucky we were to be brought up in a place like Northeast."

## Most of the Lebanese People Settled on Main and Marshall

*Don Risk Interview*

Don Risk served as a city alderman from 1961 to 1968, and on the Minneapolis Planning Commission until 1990. He is now retired from political life but sells real estate with his son. He grew up in Northeast and continues to live there with his wife Colleen. Gracious and hospitable, Don is very proud of his culture.

*Don Risk's parents Elias and Lucy Risk with Uncle Joseph George 811 Spring St NE 1955.*

"My father and mother had been farmers in the hill country of Lebanon, which was part of Turkey before World War I and part of Syria after the war. They came from the villages of Bjdrifl and Kfefan in 1915 and 1916. Like many immigrants, they were looking for a better life. When they arrived in America, they spoke no English, had only the clothes on their back and a small bag.

"My father first worked as a day laborer in Toledo, Ohio. Later, he came to Minneapolis where his good friend, Joseph George, and my father's wife-to-be, Lucy, lived. Most of the Lebanese people settled in the area of Main and Marshall Streets from East Hennepin to Broadway.

"The Henne's owned the Green Keg beer parlor above the grocery store at 603 Main Street. The brothers, Farhet and Risha, delivered pop from door to door with a truck. Later, they became the largest distributors of Grain Belt Beer, but they also delivered for the East Side Beverage Company and Miller Beer. Mary Rahana also had a grocery store. Many of the Lebanese people changed their names at Ellis Island because of the difficult pronunciation and spelling.

"I was born in 1928 in General Hospital while my family was living at 811 Spring Street. Our family was very poor. As a young boy, I used to go around with my friends looking for aluminum to sell to the peddlers. In turn, the peddlers took the metal to the scrap yard to sell.

"We used to go down to the bars with a box that had a brush, a buffing rag, and polish to shine shoes. We charged a nickel a shine. Then, we would check all the pinball machines. Often, the machines would kick out metal chips that we could use to buy candy and such. Sometimes the place would be raided, and the police would throw all the chips in the river. Later, us kids would all go out for a dive.

"My first job was setting pins at Friendly Alleys for five cents a line at the age of 13. Later, I shined shoes at London Cleaners on East Hennepin. Next door was the Doghouse, which served hot dogs and hamburgers. It was bought by Nye's Polonaise room. When I was sixteen, I worked the nightshift for Terminal Warehouse on Washington Avenue.

"The schools I went to were Webster, Sheridan, and Edison. After school I worked at J.B. Hanson's grocery

*Webster School 707 NE Monroe 1922.*

store on Monroe and Spring Street. This store was later taken over by Ben German. Fruit baskets were lined in front of the store, but mostly, I remember the ice cream cones. To this day I have never had a better one.

"During the summer my friends and I would hop a freight train and go over to Nicollet Island. The Steele Desota Ice Cream Company would throw out old ice cream packed in piles of ice, and we'd see if we could find any.

"We swam nude on the point which was across the channel from B. F. Nelson. Then, we'd hop a freight and go over to the markets on First Avenue North. Watermelons were often left on the freight cars. Sometimes, we'd go up to the loop and the Stockholm Theater on Washington. One guy would distract the ticket taker and the other six would sneak in. Then after the movie we'd hop a freight and go home.

"We used to play a lot of street hockey. There weren't so many cars back then, so we'd set up a couple of cans and try to shoot the puck between them. Another game we used to play was "kick the stick." It was a lot like tag except you had to run up and get the stick that was leaned up against the curb line. We also played "hose." which was similar to baseball except we couldn't afford a ball. We'd cut a short piece of hose and hit it with a bat. Anything hit over the telephone wire was always a home run.

"Another thing we did both for fun and necessity was go to the Great Northern station, about four or five blocks from my house. We'd go up to the coal chute where the train engines would load up, and have a race to see who could fill their gunny sack first, then run home. Sometimes, we would fill up four or five bags and hide them underneath lumber and head for home to get a sled for hauling. There was always the chance that the bags would be gone when we returned. For a bag of coal, you could get a haircut from Joe Trisco who owned a barbershop on Third and Monroe.

"Logan Park was a great place to go for skating because everybody would be there. It was wonderful. In the summer, the whole neighborhood would come out for band concerts. There would be hundreds of people there. Logan Park produced a lot of great athletes like the Cassid brothers, Tony Jaros, and Clayton Tonnamaker, guys that went to Edison and East High Vocational.

"My parents never owned an automobile. They walked or took the streetcar. The Bryant Johnson line took you all the way up to Twenty-ninth Avenue. It was always great fun to pull the trolley line in the winter time. The trolley would stop because the electric line disconnected from the cable and the conductor would have to get out and attach the line again. We thought it was great fun.

"My family shopped at East Hennepin at Ideal Drug, Woolworths, and Eklunds. You could charge almost anything, even groceries and medications. In those days, your word meant a lot. There was much more respect and integrity. If my dad said he'd pay, he would. We also only bought what we could afford.

"Our church, St. Maron's, has always been the center of activity in our lives. Many of our friends belong to this church. Our festival day is August 18, and Lebanese food, music, and crafts are featured. Social functions attended by large numbers of Lebanese rarely ended without a Dabke, an Arabic dance similar to the Greek dance where everyone joins hands.

"We celebrate holidays with a big meal. Some of the traditional Lebanese foods are kibby, ground lamb and spices mixed with cracked wheat bulgur. This can be baked or fried. Malfoof is a cabbage roll with rice, ground lamb, and tomatoes. Cusa is zucchini hollowed out and filled with lamb, rice, and spices. We eat lots of lamb, which is really better for you than beef. Homemade flat bread can be filled with meat or eaten plain with lots of butter and jam. Baklava, one of our most well known foods, consists of filo dough filled with crushed walnuts, butter and honey and then rolled. Today, Emily's Deli and Jacob's 101 serve a variety of Lebanese foods. The Holy Land Baker on Twenty-fifth and Central has the best gyros in town.

"Northeast is different than other neighborhoods, because there has been a steady stream of immigrants after World War II, and now again after the disarray in Europe, Russia, and the Middle East. It is still a flourishing community; a community filled with pride in the homes, churches, heritages, and families. It is a community that accepts and nourishes different cultures."

## On the Avenue—
## Memories of East Hennepin in the Sixties

*Carol Brecht Interview*

Carol Brecht lived in Northeast Minneapolis most of her life but recently moved to a townhouse in Blaine. One room in Carol's new home is filled with memorabilia of special moments of the past. A homer hanky and a picture of Fred Astaire and Ginger Rogers hangs on one of the walls.

*Carol with her family on the day of her baptism, taken on the steps of St. Boniface Church.*

Carol has worked in clerical and sales jobs and enjoys teaching ballroom dancing as a hobby. She recalls spending much of her teenage time on East Hennepin Avenue and has a special place in her heart for Logan Park where she learned to dance.

"I grew up on Adams Street between Spring and Summer Streets and went to St. Boniface Catholic School. My parents married in Our Lady of Lourdes church. My mother was French and my father was German. Descended from generations of printers, my father worked for the Daily Journal and Minneapolis Star.

"We were aware of being German and stood out, mostly because of going to a German school. We knew we lived in Polish territory, but still felt very much a part of the community.

"One of my uncles worked for the Grain Belt Brewery, and when my aunt visited from California, my whole family would go on the Grain Belt tour and make a day of it. I remember the wooden barrels, tall ceilings, and clean floors. The grounds had deer and pretty waterfalls. Afterwards, we picnicked with munchies and beer, compliments of the beer company.

"There was a time when East Hennepin Avenue was packed with stores. If my two sisters and I couldn't get downtown, then shopping on the avenue was the next best thing.

"We liked going to Emil's Shoe Store. A big green paper parrot hung over the display counter. First, Emil would bring out the metal shoesizer and determine our sizes. Then, he'd bring out lots of different shoes, while he cracked jokes. I remember Emil had a crewcut, and he looked and acted like Gary Moore. Paul Parrot shoes were the popular shoes of the day. When we made the final purchase, Emil would wrap the

*S and L Department Store and Griffin Drug 400 Central Ave. 1936.*

shoebox in brown paper, tie it with string, and hand it to us, along with a lollipop, as we went out the door.

"We loved the S & L Store, which had three floors filled with merchandise. Every year we went there for our fall wardrobe. My mother made most of our clothes, so it was a treat to have a few store-bought items. School uniforms were sold on the second floor. I loved going there, because it was like a gramma's attic with rickety old steps. The floor was filled with unique items especially for children. The Horst Education building is there now.

"Ideal Drug used to be next to Emil's Shoe Store but moved over to Eastgate Mall across the street. Wednesday was coupon day at Ideal Drug. The White Castle was on Fourth Street and East Hennepin, but was recently moved to Thirty-third Street and Lyn-

dale Avenue. This was the first White Castle in the state and the owners wanted to preserve the building. We went there for lunch when we shopped on the avenue. The Eastgate Shopping Center consisted of Red Owl, Doyles, McNamara's Sports Bar, Ideal Drug, and Leibs, an expensive women's store. Doyles was the hot spot for teens and well-known for delicious fried

*White Castle 329 Central Ave. 1954.*

chicken and the best french fries in town. The fries were served on a huge tray. We used to stop there on the way home from De La Salle High School dances on Friday nights.

"The Factory Outlet Store was a great place across from the Eastgate Shopping Center. It was filled with good stuff like knickknacks, kitchen items and unfinished furniture. We once bought an unfinished phone desk there to replace our gossip bench.[11] There was also an F.W. Woolworths dime store and three furniture stores in the shopping center. Plain or flowered rainbonnets were ten cents at the checkout at Woolworth's. There were also lots of Goodie hair ornaments, nail polish, and cheap *Evening in Paris* perfume. Jim's Coffee House, the one made famous in the movie "Untamed Heart," is across from where White Castle used to be.

"Another store that my mother really loved was the Columbia Department Store. The salesclerk who always helped her was named Lillian. Another store located on the avenue going toward the island was the Doll Hospital, which had all kinds of darling dolls in the window. They did a beautiful job of fixing up dolls. I had my doll's hair fixed there, because it was damaged from wear and tear of being played with so much. Babyland was also a unique place. I remember the sign advertising their logo had big letters in pastel colors above the entrance. They mostly had baby furniture, like white wicker cribs, bassinets, and other baby gadgets. It was fun to go by there and look in the big window.

"Sometimes if we got bored with East Hennepin on our Saturday trips, we'd go up to Central Avenue for a little variety, looking for bigger and better shops up there. Although the walk was refreshing, we usually didn't find anything on Central Avenue that we couldn't get on East Hennepin. One of the best memories I have of Central Avenue is of the Sun Drive-In. I didn't go there all the time, but the times I did were really great. Groups of friends hung out there' but nobody caused trouble. We would go from car to car just to 'shoot the breeze'. What I really remember was the Sun Burger, which was made according to a secret recipe. There was nothing like that Sun Burger in the whole city of Minneapolis. It was so-o-o good! I understand the Sun Saloon in Northeast Minneapolis still serves the original recipe.

"Sometimes, we went across the bridge and walked over to Nicollet Island. At that time, Nicollet Island was pretty run down. There were coffee shops, delis, antique shops, and flop houses. East Hennepin and Nicollet Island were totally different cultures. Many people said, 'The bridge made all the difference.'

"The Salvation Army Store was a great place to buy old books or knickknacks for a nickel. My father took the family out for a drive on holidays, and we would sometimes see the bums waiting in the soup line. It was a little scary but, in some ways, had a mystique. When we got back across the bridge on the East Hennepin side and closer to Broadway, we would give a sigh of relief. We were safe and back in our own neighborhood again."

---

11. A gossip bench had a small table with an attached seat on the side meant for the person speaking on the telephone.

# Life on the Soo Line

*Charles I. Snelson Interview*

The Soo Line Railroad employed Charles Snelson for thirty-seven years. He began on the cement gang in Superior, Wisconsin and later, worked on the bridge and building crew. Finally, he served as a brakeman, conductor and switchman at the Shoreham yard on

*Charles Snelson 1956.*

Twenty-eighth and Central Avenues from 1954 to 1987. He is now retired and lives with his wife Aileen in Columbia Heights. In 1954, when Snelson started, thousands of employees worked for Soo Line as engineers, electricians, section men, roundhouse workers, officials, clerks, and office personnel. Although he enjoys retirement, Charles remembers life on the Soo Line fondly.

"Soo Line was a big influence on the Northeast community, providing employment for a great number of people. Lots of houses in Northeast Minneapolis are built out of box car lumber. The houses that once cost $5,000 to $6,000 dollars sell for $90,000. Some conductors never drove a car, because they always walked to work. And some people say there used to be a lake where the Shoreham yard is today.

"I was fortunate to work for Soo Line, because they were a family-type company. I made many close friends over the years. I started out making $13 per 100 miles which was about equal to eight hours. When I retired I was making $110 for 100 miles. Every brakeman was paid the same, regardless of how long they worked there.

"I worked at the Shoreham yard as a head man. As the saying goes, 'Wherever the engine goes, the head-man has to be close by.' The brakemen crew consisted of two men on caboose, the conductor, rear brakeman, one on the head and, sometimes, a third brakeman. The hand signs we used on the line were very important and were our only way of communicating. The most important sign was stop, but there were hundreds of others that we had to learn. We had our own language that an outsider wouldn't understand. Kick, drop, matching hand-sign, housetrack, passing train, mainline, creamery track, small town. We had to learn them all. There could be an accident if you didn't know the right sign.

"Soo Line was a good place to work, and the overall attitude of employees was good. They allowed time off

for health reasons or injuries. In fact, they insisted that you take at least six weeks off for recovery. The benefits were not very good. But later, medical, more vacation, holidays, and away from home expenses became standard benefits as the unions became more powerful. Strikes were not often and never lasted long because of the Presidential Emergency Board. Railroads were essential to the whole U. S. If the railroad stopped, the whole country stopped. The longest strike Soo Line ever had was during the summer of 1994 and was not nationwide.

"All the guys had nicknames. The trainmen were Swede, Snoos, and Tom Cat. The engineers went by Haggar, Ding Dong, Hook (not to his face), Corporal, Chief, Hardhead, Fisheye, Long Belly, Gramma, Preacher, Sugar Lips, and Juice. Juice's nickname came when he misunderstood a waitress' question. She asked, 'Do you want soup or juice?'

'What kind of juice is that—super juice?' he said.

"The men had to have their pocket watches approved by the railroad. We checked the time in the morning against the designated company clock in the

*Soo Line Locomotive #600 in 1900.*

*Shoreham Yard storm damage scene shows railway car shops and round house, St. Anthony Cemetery in background 1941.*

Shoreham yard office. The watches were inspected once a month by an inspector at Gustafson Jewelry. I bought my gold Hamilton at a hockshop in 1954 in downtown Minneapolis for $25.00.

"The Shoreham yard was divided into the A and B yard with about 20–25 tracks in each yard. Then, there was the roundhouse, the Soo shops, the repair shops, the tin shops, the boxcar, the brake shop and the painting shed.

"Working as a trainman or brakeman was a dangerous occupation. You had to be alert. At any time, you could be pinned by an engine. My job was to ride on top or on the side of the car, hopping from car to car, even in ice, snow, wind, or rain. Overhead bridges

could also be a hazard. Also, there were more injuries during fog. I watched many accidents happen over the years.

"There was a first aid man at Shoreham during the day and a company doctor. The injured men were usually taken to Northwestern Hospital.

"The cold could become extreme, so we had to keep moving. Wearing good clothing was a must: long underwear, mobile boots, good wool lined overshoes, chopper mittens,[12] a good cap with earflaps, and a parka.

"We had to be prepared for anything at anytime, and any kind of weather. At times, we couldn't even get a plow out. Many storms tied up the whole system. Often, there was nothing to do but wait it out. Sometimes, we were snowed in for days at a time.

"There were lots of hobos hanging around at Shoreham yard. They rode the trains often, mostly in the empty box cars. Soo Line didn't want them around but didn't take much action to stop them. Sometimes, the Soo Line Police Department would take a bum off a train and drive them over to Central or University Avenue. But by the time the policeman got back to the yard, the same bum was back again in the boxcar. So many of them had nowhere to go. Sometimes, the men would feed them. They were a little scary sometimes, but they were usually harmless.

"Once, I was walking down the track checking the brakes on the boxcars. I was all alone on a blacker than tar night, when all of a sudden, I heard this booming voice say "Hey, young fella, where dir train

_____
12. Oversized leather mittens lined with heavy wool.

going?" My skin turned inside out. He was a big fella. It took me a minute to answer.

"This train is going to Glenwood," I told him

"Where's Glenwood?" he asked.

I told him where it was then he said, "I got to get off dis train."

"He scared the devil out of me and after that I was a lot more cautious.

"Lodging on the road was tough. Small towns like Dresser, Junction, Barron, Superior, and Glenwood could be less than desirable. Most of these had only one place to stay and one restaurant. After working sixteen hours, we would head off to find a place to sleep. I slept in the caboose many times. One time in Superior, I went to bed and woke up with a whole flock of pigeons that had moved in with me from the window sill. In Glenwood, at the Sam Parker House Hotel, the shower handle fell off and almost scalded me. Later, the toilet or shower broke in the upstairs sleeping room and the water came through the ceiling and dripped on our heads while we were eating.

"At the Weyerhauser Hotel in Wisconsin, the rooms were dirty and had poor mattresses. It looked like they only swept once a month, and the lights had cords hanging down. There wasn't good heat to begin with, and the wind would blow right through the windows. Once, during a blizzard a man came in from outside. As a joke, someone asked "What room did you come out of? We all laughed our heads off.

"We worked seven days a week. We wouldn't see our family for a week at a time. We'd go home for only eight hours and have to go back to work again. If the railroad was short of men, you worked or you were fired, regardless of weather, night, day, or holiday.

There were lots of holidays away from home, sometimes with no extra pay.

"We were always on call. If they called, you had 90 minutes to get there. The engineers and trainmen were called most often. One old-time engineer of 40 years was called and he said, "I'm not going to work." They told him he had to. He said, "I'm not going to, I quit." Not much notice, they said. "All my life, I only had 90 minutes," he answered.

"There were many home parties and local union parties. We rented a hall with music and beer. One party was at the New Brighton fire hall. There was also an annual Christmas party at the VFW on Twenty-sixth and Central. These were both for retired and active members. Annual picnics were also given by the Soo Employees Association for all Soo Line employees.

"Since the early days, there has been a 180 degree turn around. Steam engines changed over to diesel and electric in about 1953. Two-way radios made a big difference, because the workers no longer needed hand signals. In recent years, Soo Line bought the Milwaukee Railroad and the M. N. & S. The many unions consolidated into the United Transportation Union. Some freight trains now run with one engineer and one conductor. The yard crews that consisted of about 2,000 employees, now use one or two men. There used to be an agent or operator about every three to five miles and a dispatcher in every town. Now, the depots are all gone.

Although Charles retired from his work, his connection to the railroad community is as vital as ever. He and his wife participate in three railroad clubs. The Soo Line Old Timers meet five times a year and

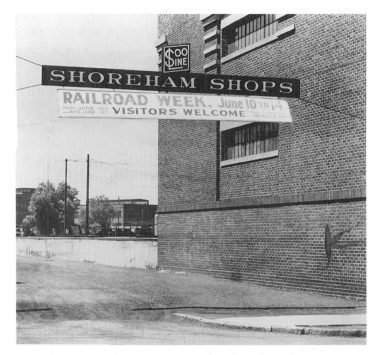

*Soo Shops open house as part of railroad week in 1935.*

the Snelson's get together between those occasions with some of the members for dinner, card playing, or bingo. The Soo Line Vets also convene regularly and publish a newsletter that recounts memories, trips, and other announcements of interest to retired employees, while the Soo Line Silver Rails gather each and every month. The railroad is definitely in Charles' blood.

## We Learned in German and English at St. Boniface

*Wilfred Leitschuh Interview*

Wilfred Leitschuh is now retired from managing the Leitschuh Insurance Agency, which his father established in 1915. He and his wife Harriet have lived in the same house in Northeast Minneapolis for forty years. Their house is a brick rambler with salmon-colored geraniums in the front window box and a four season porch that looks out at carefully sculpted vegetable and flower gardens. Red poppies, yellow daisies, and white alyssum frame a birdbath. The couple's shared affection for gardening and history is evident from the surroundings.

"My mother's family came from Germany when she was six months old, and my father's family was from New Ulm. My grandfather was a blacksmith in a shop on Eighth and Marshall Streets, where Elsie's Bowling Alley is now. He was a wagon maker and shod horses for the city of Minneapolis. My father came to Minnesota in 1875.

"In 1912, the year I was born, my family lived at 113 Broadway near Jacob's 101 Restaurant. Later, my father built a duplex at 415 Eighth Avenue. It was a Spanish-style house with a red roof and still stands today. I lived there until I was married.

"I delivered papers from the time I was in sixth grade until I graduated from De La Salle High School. My route was from Broadway Avenue to Eighth Avenue and Fifth Street down to the river. I had forty-five daily papers and 100 Sunday papers to deliver. I walked and pulled a wagon or sled. Later, I rode my

*Wilfred (right) and his brother Edmund Leitschuh 1913.*

bike. I got paid $20.00 a month. Once a month I had to go out and collect the money and every week I had to go out and solicit orders. The daily paper was 45 cents per month, and the Sunday paper was twenty-five cents. Seventy cents then was like $7 in today's money. Often, the papers were dumped on the corner, and kids would come by and steal them. They would sell them downtown. I would have to order new papers and pay for the stolen ones.

"We stayed mostly in the area where we lived because we had everything we needed and rarely went beyond that. There was a time when Central Avenue seemed like a foreign country. It was called New Boston. There was no Broadway back then. The Main Street Theater on Eleventh Avenue and Main Street had silent pictures back in the war years when I was in grade school. Westerns with stars like Tom Mix were popular. The organist would play music to go along with the horse movement and other sounds. Cowboy and Indian shows cost ten cents. Sometimes a rat would run across your feet during the movie. The Mengelkoch Hide and Tallow Company was a half a block away from the theater. Animals that died were brought there. That probably attracted the rats.

"I had a friend that was an attorney working for the Gluek Brewery. He had the nickname of "Lightning" because he knew how to make good beer. My uncle Jack also worked there on the loading dock. Back then they loaded everything manually. The brewery was plagued with river rats, so they hired my Uncle Joe to come over and shoot them with his BB gun. Upstairs was a beer garden that served free beer. People drank at the big wooden bar and played cards at the tables, and chairs that were set up. All of the tavern owners in those days were bootleggers. My uncle Jack used to bring leftover beer home with him. Most of the breweries had baseball teams, too. My dad managed a baseball team for one of the breweries.

"Some of the foods we ate in those days were country sausage, which was only made in the fall. The German butcher shop was Vos on the corner of Fifth and Marshall. The Polish butcher shop was Krawczyk's on Seventh and Marshall, which later moved to Lowry Avenue and Second Street. The meat was kept in salt brine because there was no refrigeration back then. My family shopped at Eklund's Men's Store and Mergen's Dry Goods. Sometimes we would get shoes or skates for Christmas.

"My father wouldn't eat pork because he had eaten so much salt pork. Back then, headcheese with vinegar was a delicacy. I still like it today. And my mother buried carrots in sand in our basement to keep them fresh. We had lots of sauerkraut and German potato salad. Women competed to make the best potato salad. My mother baked bread twice a week, in the middle of the week and on Saturday. We had eight children in our family, and all of us fought for the crust.

"In the evening, my parents would leave out a fresh loaf of bread and butter. When my friends came over, we would all sit around and eat bread and butter. My mother also made streusel and potato pancakes. We would eat herring and peaches together. After Mass, we would stop at the bakery on Broadway and Adams. We would order three streusel coffee cakes for 10 cents each. Then, we'd have hot cocoa with marshmallow cream on top.

"There wasn't a lot for kids to do in the wintertime, so we did a lot of skating at Sheridan and Logan Parks where there was a hut with a stove and benches. We didn't have to worry about anybody stealing our shoes, because we wore clamp on skates. We went tobogganing at Columbia Park. One year we had a special slide made of pure ice and built it up on the sides. A bunch of us would pile on the toboggan and wrap our legs around each other. I loved the part at the bottom where you would hit the air. Unfortunately I broke my nose once while I was tobagganing.

"Lots of people in lower Northeast worked at B. F. Nelson. At night, I remember that the waste of recycled rags would be blown out of the chimneys. Dust would cover the porches and window sills in the morning. People complained a lot and there were more fires there than any other company, probably because of so much paper. The firemen would often just leave their hoses. Once, two fire trucks collided on Eighth Avenue and Sibley Streets. One was coming South on Sibley and the other down Eighth Avenue. They couldn't hear each other coming because of all the noise. The horses scrambled and one of the firemen was killed.

"I remember the smell of the Gedney Pickle Factory located on Lowry Avenue and the river. The Kullberg Manufacturing Company on Sixth Avenue and Main Street had steam whistles that they blew every day at noon and 6:00 in the evening. You could set your watch by it. Sometimes, the whistle would blow on festive occasions, too. At the end of World War I, all the companies in town blew their steam whistles. People really celebrated on that day. Many tied tin cans on their cars and drove up and down the streets.

"We also had a curfew whistle that blew every night at nine o'clock. All of us kids would run like hell to get home if we heard that whistle. I don't know of anyone that ever got caught after curfew, but there was always the threat hanging over your head.

"The Leitschuh family belonged to St. Boniface Catholic Church and went to school there. We learned our catechism, reading, and spelling in both German and English. St. Boniface had a three-lane bowling alley in the basement with no automatic pin setter. Sunday afternoons we would always bowl. We'd stop bowling for vespers at 3:00 and continue bowling after. Some kids went on to be pretty noted bowlers in the community. Our church was originally named St. Bonifacius but, during the war, it was renamed St. Boniface. We had to take the letters off the school. I remember one Irish family wouldn't let me walk on their sidewalk. And someone reported my dad as a German spy.

"We had the Zenith Dramatic Club at St. Boniface. There were three plays every week on Sunday and Monday. Some of our actors also filled in at the Schubert Theater downtown. Our directors were Al Mauren, Albert Wilwerding and Norbert Henkes. It was my job to sell tickets. We even had some reserved seats.

The ice depot was on Sixteenth Avenue and Third Street. Later, Kroger's Grocery Store was opened in the same spot. It has since become Rainbow Foods. There was Appleton Grocery Store owned by a Jewish family on Eighth Avenue and Marshall that raised chickens in their backyard. They sold bakery goods for half price on Sunday mornings. Joe and Ann's Restaurant was on Second and Broadway Avenue. It started out as Mrs. Smith's Grocery. There was a showcase behind glass and everything was sold in bulk. Then, they started making sandwiches and pies and it turned into a restaurant.

"I worked in my dad's office at the Leitschuh Insurance agency for 50 years. I started out with odd jobs, collecting accounts and teaching myself to type on a manual typewriter. It was hard to sell insurance during the Depression years. My dad also started a mortgage business. In those days, the only way you could get money for a house was to borrow it or take out a contract for deed. My father worked six days and six

*Leitschuh Insurance Agency in 1915 known as Sulflow and Maas.*

evenings. I did the same when I started in the business. I retired in 1982.

"My wife's family lived at the end of the streetcar line on Twenty-eighth and Grand Street. Her family once had a farm and raised potatoes on the land that was later sold to NSP. Her father, Anthony Reiners owned a team of horses and plowed the sidewalks for the city of Minneapolis. He also pulled the yellow sprinkler wagon that cleaned the streets. Before the streets were paved there was a lot of upkeep involved. If we didn't have rain, they had to be sprinkled every few days to keep the dust down. I remember all of us kids would run behind the wagon to cool off in summer.

Today, Wilfred and Harriet spend their time gardening and enjoying the company of their five children and eleven grandchildren. They like to play cards and have cook outs on the weekends. And take turns having special holiday dinners with all the trimmings. They like to include some of the favorites that their mothers made—old fashioned pickled beets, date nut bread, pumpkin pie from scratch and German potato salad. They are active in the church and the community and feel fortunate to have grown up in a neighborhood that is filled with good people.

## It Is Better to Light Just One Candle In the Darkness Than to Curse the Darkness

*Ivan Olson Interview*
Reprinted with permission of Project Challenge [1978?]

I was born August, 1900 in Sundvall, Sweden. I came here 56 years ago and for 45 years have lived here on the same corner of Pierce and 22nd in "Northeast" Minneapolis, U.S.A.

Sundvall was a sawmill district with a climate similar to Minnesota's. There was not enough work for the people. We could hunt and fish, but we did not have

*Ivan Olson at his home on Pierce Street.*

enough food to eat. We seldom had meat or eggs. Mother would bake hardtack for us. We would make coffee with ½ and ½—coffee beans and roasted oats. It made the coffee last longer.

My father's friend went to Minneapolis, Minnesota in America as a young man. When I decided to go also I remember the last night in Sweden with my brother, sister and Ma and Pa. Pa said, "You are going out alone now. You must have a friend to go to." He gave me an address and some advice. "Let me warn you, it is rough out there in the world, you will get cheated. Remember if you get cheated once it's the guy's fault. If you get cheated twice, it's your fault. Regardless of what country you come to, if you are not an honest man, you will not be a good citizen anywhere in the world."

When I came to Minneapolis and looked up this friend, he had worked his way up to chief engineer at Swedish Hospital. I was lucky to get my first job as a fireman at Swedish. I received room and board and $60 a month. I felt like a king. There were other Swedes at work, too. On the night shift, for the first month, I worked with an Englishman named Snowbank who taught me the English language by using old magazines. My wife and daughter continue to correct my English. I'm still learning every day.

The greatest moment in my life was when I married an American girl in 1925. We've been married for 53 years. After we were first married, we moved to Chicago where I worked on a construction job building a 35-story building. That building would look like an outhouse compared to what they build today. Back then we thought it was a skyscraper.

When I came back to Minneapolis, I started work-

ing for Pioneer Engineering on Fifteenth and Central as a tool and dye maker and worked there for 36 years. They sent me to school. I worked for 45 cents an hour during the Depression. I was lucky. When I quit 12 years ago, I had the longest record of service. I tell you, some days, I think we are living in heaven compared to the black days of the Depression. I remember an empty ice box and a cold stove. The winter of '34 was the worst. Thirty-seven per cent of the people were working and the rest were not. Potatoes were 37 cents a bushel. There is an old Swedish saying that helped us make it, "It is better to light just one little candle in the darkness than to curse the darkness." I tell you, we've come a long way since then.

There is something to be said about my house, too. I have painted it four or five times. It is made of birchwood. It was built 68 years ago at the wage of 32 cents an hour. I bought it for $5,000.00 and now it is worth $69,000.00, they tell me. I can't think of a better place to spend 43 years under the sun like here on this corner.

I have been here two thirds of my life. I am so proud to be an American. God help the guy and woman that is not proud of being an American. I would like my dying words from my lips to be that I love being an American.

I still remember the horsedrawn milk wagons every morning. Sidewalks were plowed with horses but they had to stop plowing the sidewalks that way when the square cement blocks were installed because the horses would wreck them. So they passed an ordinance to shovel our own sidewalks.

My wife, who grew up three blocks from Prescott School, still remembers when the place where our house is now was a cornfield. From Lowry to Broadway and Central to Stinson were the city limits. Beyond that was all farmland.

A great day for my wife's family was to pack up a lunch and walk from Buchanan Street for five miles to Lake Johanna. They would rent a boat for 25 cents and fish all day. At night they would walk home with gunny sacks full of sunfish and crappies. Let me say, they had a heck of a nice time too. Today I can drive 300 miles with a car and think nothing of it. I don't

*Prescott School 1024 Lowry Ave NE 1909.*

even have to use my legs if I don't want to. We have come such a long way. Sometimes I call myself a "spoiled brat." I tell you the only song I sing is that I love America.

I remember during an election when the Swedes and Norwegians couldn't get together. One was a

Democrat and the other a Republican. Minutes before the election, good neighbors would be standing with fists at each other's noses ready to fight. Following the election they were just as good neighbors as before, until the next election. That's how we built up America, I'm sure. I mentioned togetherness. You know, we could go a little deeper and call it love. Let us call it that. We sure need a heck of a lot of it in today's life.

Yes, I remember when we were all immigrants. It took me a year to understand street speech. All the neighbors knew each other by name. Everyone spoke his own language. They used to call the east part of Central Avenue "New Boston." I don't really know why, but they did. There were a lot of Swedes and Norwegians that lived there.

They used to call the newcomers "Greenhorns." There were so many ethnics in those days. American neighbors and people at work went out of their way to help us learn the language. This is some melting pot—this America. It is like a pot of soup. Naturally when you mix up that many ingredients, like all the immigrants who came by the Statue of Liberty, you are bound to get some kind of a funny mixture that will disrupt the beautiful taste of America, but it is the essence and this beautiful soup that is called America. It's remarkable! It is so remarkable!

I wish I could speak to the youngsters of today. If they only knew what a great country they have been lucky enough to be born in. There are some people who are trying to destroy and undermine the liberty of our country. "Don't ask what your country can do for you but what you can do for your country." I can only sing one song and that is, time and again, that I love America."

## If You Mistreat A Foreign Person, Don't Come Home

*Mama D Interview*

*Mama D in front of her house.*

How can I describe Mama D? Hardworking, spiritual, charming and delightful. At eighty years of age she is more active than most thirty year olds. She opened her first restaurant with her son, Sam, at the University of Minnesota's Dinkytown in 1965 where she fell in love with the hippies. Since then she has become well known for her restaurants in the Twin Cities. When I went to her restaurant in Eden Prairie, they were getting ready for the 11:00 buffet. I found Mama D scurrying around setting tables. She was wearing a soft polyester print dress. "Sit down, I'll get you some coffee," she said. As I plugged in my tape recorder and made myself comfortable, I looked into her smiling eyes. Her snow white hair was worn short and very stylish with a pretty widow's peak. "Tell me about your neighborhood and why your parents settled there?" was my first question.

"I grew up in the Italian section of NE, otherwise known as Dogtown (so nicknamed because of the number of dogs that ran the streets). I lived there for twenty-five years. My father came over with his two uncles in 1897 when he was fourteen years old. He was from San Giovanni in Fiore, a city in southern Italy that is southeast of Naples. He came with his uncle who was in charge of a Soo Line railroad crew, working there for several years, first in Colorado and finally in Minnesota where he settled as a young man. His uncle and my mother's uncle got to know one another and arranged the wedding between them. My father wrote to her in Italy and they courted through the mail. On the day she arrived in 1911, they were married by a justice of the peace in downtown Minneapolis. He was twenty-eight and she was only sixteen. Their marriage lasted sixty-four years.

"Neither of my Italian parents spoke English well and I did not learn it myself until I was nine years old. It was rough when I started school. The language barrier affected our ability to comprehend all that was going on in the classroom. Many of the questions the

teachers asked were lost on me. We spoke Italian at home, and we contended with English mainly at school. Some teachers made little or no attempt to help us understand.

"At Pierce School, every Christmas season, the pupils were asked in a questionnaire what they had received for Christmas the year before. My list would be the longest because I did not want anyone to know that I had not received much. On the last day before Christmas the teachers distributed gifts, one to each pupil. I was always given a book. I wanted a doll or some other toy, but because I wrote such long lists the teachers assumed that I had no need for toys. I tried not to show my disappointment and cried all the way home.

"The only doll I remember receiving was from a stranger on a hot summer day in the Great Northern Depot. My mother and I had walked into the depot to cool off when I was four or five years old. We were strolling slowly when suddenly an old man called to me. When we went over to him he opened his suitcase and took out a doll dressed in a bright red sweater with white buttons. She had real hair and eyes that opened and closed. He handed it to me and smiled. 'This is for you,' he said with a smile. I treasured the doll all through my childhood. I never knew who the old man was. Perhaps he was a relative or someone my parents knew, perhaps not. But he brought immeasurable joy that day.

"My five sisters and I were all sent to school dressed in the Italian fashion of long braids and lacy dresses that hung well below our knees. My mother clung to the old styles. I was much darker skinned than the other children in our family. This must have

*Family Portrait 1930 Mama D is on far right.*

looked very strange to the Scandinavian, German and Irish families who came earlier and were more Americanized.

"Whenever my mother was away from home, she needed an interpreter. Except for the ethnic Italian section of Northeast, the new land was alien to her. Shopping was a trauma for her at first, but she developed simple ways of communicating. If she needed soap, she took a bar from home to show the merchant. She would take a five or ten dollar bill to the store and because she didn't understand the value of the coinage, she accumulated a lot of change that she put away in a can. Although she eventually learned enough English to carry on a basic conversation, she never did learn it fluently. I can remember the warning my mother gave to me, 'If you see a foreign person and you mistreat them, don't come home.'

"The people in our neighborhood were all from the same region in Italy called Callabria. Some came from

West Virginia and some were from Cumberland. All the families knew one another: the Sellaros, the Scalices, the Ferraras, the Vescios, the Alevators, the Locascios, the Shrimpes, the Iaquintos, and the Spanos with their grocery store on the corner of Buchanan and Spring.

"This store, where people bought much of their food, was virtually the center of the neighborhood. The father, George Spano was the proprietor and the unofficial mayor of our community. His brother had a brick oven in the back of the place where he baked bread. That bread was the tastiest I ever had as a child.

"In those days the women talked on the doorsteps, you could hear Italian spoken all at once. Dogs roamed the streets without leashes and children used to steal chips of ice from the iceman. We never locked our doors, we just walked into our neighbor's house and they would put the coffee on. If someone had a baby, the neighbor would automatically go to the door with a chicken under the arm. If someone was sick, you'd bring a pot of chicken soup. Chicken soup was the penicillin of that time.

"If my mother didn't see your mother she'd make me go to your house and I didn't even have the courtesy of knocking, I'd walk right in and say, "Miss so and so, my mother hasn't seen you lately, are you all right? She'd say Honey, tell your mother that I'm fine. I just have been busy."

"Mrs. Margaret Barry founded a settlement house for the Italians in Northeast at Broadway and Pierce Streets. She developed a clinic for teachers so they could understand the Italian community and its problems. At the Margaret Barry house, I learned to play

*Taken in front of Margaret Barry House.*

tennis. I also developed an interest in reading and improving myself culturally. A young teacher named Miss Ford encouraged many of us to express ourselves in writing and acting. I wrote a short play and in a newspaper article about the settlement house I was mentioned as an actress and a playwright.

"One day in 1928, when I was fourteen, Mrs. Barry gave each of us a ticket to an athletic or cultural event. I wanted to see something I had never seen before, so I opted for the concert. I walked from Northeast to the University campus, wearing a simple white dress and sat between two people in formal evening wear. At intermission I walked among the people and marveled. I imagine they wondered how someone like me could afford a ticket. I did not understand the music, but seeing a live orchestra was exciting.

"The old neighborhood was changed by the freeway construction in 1971. Many houses were razed or removed from the area bounded by Johnson Street and Buchanan, East Hennepin and Broadway Avenue. When people had to give up their homes and be relocated to a strange part of town, they died not long afterward. They were once a big family spread out over several city blocks and that was a source of strength. The world they knew was gone forever.

"As it turned out, the freeway did not require that our house be taken but only most of the backyard garden. My mother accepted it as a fact of life, and of course, she and my father were paid for the land. When the highway work began, the garden was in full bloom and would not be ready to be picked for another two or three weeks. My mother managed to get the construction workers to delay tearing out her garden until it had been harvested. Today the Italian neighborhood is only half its former size. Beyond this, it is like a cemetery. All I have left is the memory of this fine old neighborhood."

# Bibliography

"A Diamond in the Rough, Sheridan Neighborhood's Grain Belt Brewery." *Preservation Matters,* Aug 1986.

Amundson, Roland C. "Listen to the Bottle Say "Gluek, Gluek, Gluek." *Hennepin History*, Winter 1988–89.

Anderson, Brian. "Mayslack's: Beef and Ethnic Trimmings. " *Minneapolis Star and Tribune Picture Magazine*, 8 April 1973.

Ashmore, Margo. "Hoofers to Help Celebrate Hollywood Theater's History and Maybe-Future." *Northeaster,* 24 Feb 1993.

Batson, Larry. "Blackey's Bakery." *Minneapolis Tribune* 5 Jan 1980.

Becerra, Marilyn. "Nordeast." *Minneapolis Tribune* 7 Sept 1969.

Binkard, Betty. "Northeast: Ethnic Heritage and Modern Changes." *Insight Magazine*, 14 June 1978.

——"Northeast built on Pride, Care and Hard Work." Insight Magazine 31 May 1978.

Bolin, Winifred Wandersee. "Heating Up the Melting Pot." *Minnesota History*, Summer 1976.

Borchert, John R., David Gephard, David Lanegran, and Judith A. Martin. *Legacy Of Minneapolis*. Engle Cliffs, NJ: Prentice Hall, 1983.

Boxmeyer, Don, "Al's Place" *St. Paul Pioneer Press,* 3 March 1991.

Bromley, Edward A. Minneapolis Portrait of the Past. Minneapolis: Voyageur Press. 1973.

Carr, David. "Singing In the Rain: A Tour of Northeast." *Twin Cities Reader* 12 Oct 1983.

Chmielewski, Edward A. "History of Holy Cross Parish: A Polish American Community, 1886–1914." Master's thesis, St. Paul Seminary 1959.

*Church of Holy Cross Centennial Parish Book, 1886–1986.* Minneapolis.

*Church of St. Cyril's: 90th Anniversary Parish Booklet* 1981. Minneapolis.

Clark, Clifford E., Ed. Minnesota in a Century of Change. St. Paul: Minnesota Historical Society Press, 1989.

Clements, Amy I. "Grain Belt Brewery Tour Illuminates Northeast Building's Colorful History." *Northeaster,* 24 Sept 1986.

——"St.Anthony of Padua Church is Mother Church of the Lakes." *Northeaster*, 30 July 1986.

——"Holy Cross Celebrates 100th," *Northeaster* 10 Sept 1986.

*Cream of Wheat. Adding Warmth to Mornings for 100 years: Cream of Wheat*. Minneapolis 1993.

Crown Iron Works. Crown Iron Works Centennial 1878–1978. Minneapolis. Hennepin County History Center 1978.

*Elim Baptist Church Centennial Directory.* 1988.

Emanuel Evangelical Lutheran Parish book. 1944.

Fleming, Fredric J. "A History of the Parish of St. Anthony of Padua." Master's thesis, St. Paul Seminary 1955.

Fuehrer, Tim. "Early Edison: Vaudeville, Popcorn, Sunlight Dances, Sodas at Schrags." *Northeaster,* 17 May 1989.

Gedney Pickle Company. *Welcome to M. A. Gedney Co*. Minneapolis, 1992.

Gelbach, Deborah L. *From this Land: A History of Minnesota's Empires, Enterprises*. Northridge, CA: Windsor Publications, 1988.

Germundsen, Doug. "Everyone in Nordeast Knows Tony." *Post-East Edition*, 28 June 1978.

Gianetti, Louis and Scott Eyman. *Flashback: A Brief History of Film.* Englewood Cliffs, NJ: Prentice Hall, 1986.

Hage, Dave. "The Neighborhood's Not the Same Anymore." *Mpls.St. Paul,* April 1982.

——"The Casey Stengel of Northeast." *Mpls.St. Paul,* April 1982.

Holcombe R.I. and William H. Bingham. *Compendium of History & Biography of Minneapolis and Hennepin County.* Chicago: H. Taylor & Co., 1914.

Holmquist, June Drenning. *They Chose Minnesota: A Survey of the States Ethnic Groups.* St. Paul: Minnesota Historical Society Press. 1981.

"Josephine Reshetar, 76, Restaurateur Since 1932." *Star-Tribune* 11 Feb 1991.

Kane, Lucille. *The Waterfall that Built A City; The Falls of St. Anthony in Minneapolis.* St. Paul: Minnesota Historical Society Press. 1966.

Martin, Frank and Carole Zellie. "The Development of Neighborhood Movie Theaters in Minneapolis, 1910–1945." Minneapolis Heritage Preservation Commission.

Martin, Judith A. *Where We Live: Residential Districts of Minneapolis and St. Paul.* St. Paul: University of Minnesota Press. 1983.

McMillan, Connie. "The Old-Time Family Butcher Shop." *Mpls.St. Paul* Sept 1978.

Meier, Peg. "A Taste of Italy in Minneapolis." *Star Tribune* 8 June 1975.

Minneapolis Aquatennial Association and the Minneapolis Centennial Committee. *Minneapolis, City of Opportunity: A Century of Progress in the Aquatennial City.* Minneapolis: T. S. Denison & Co., 1956.

*Minneapolis Golden Jubilee* 1867–1917 Minneapolis Public Library Special Collections, 1917.

Morrow, Barry. "The Beltrami Neighborhood Remembered." *Common Ground* Spring 1974.

"Northeast, A History." Sun Newspapers Inc. Bloomington 1976.

Northrup King. One Hundred Years of Trust 1884–1984.

O'Brien, Frank G. "Skating Pleasures of Early Days." *in Minnesota Pioneer Sketches.* Minneapolis: Housekeeper Press 1904.

Olson, Mary Ellen. "The Ethnic Mix of Hennepin County." *Hennepin County History.* Summer 1987.

*One Hundred Years: The Centennial History of St. Boniface. 1858–1958.* Minneapolis.

O'Neill, Rev.Edward. *History of Hennepin County and City of Minneapolis.* Minneapolis: Northstar Publishing, 1881. Reprint, Walsworth 1976.

Our Lady of Lourdes Parish Book. *Notre Dame De Minneapolis—The French Canadian Catholics* 1977.

Pine, Carol. *Northern States People: NSP The Past 70 Years.* St. Paul: North Central Publishing, 1979.

Reardon, James. *The Catholic Church in the Diocese of St. Paul.* St. Paul: North Central Publishing 1952.

*St. Anthony Falls Rediscovered Architectural Heritage.* Minneapolis Riverfront Development Board Coordination. 1980.

*St. Anthony of Padua: 125th Anniversary Parish Booklet.* 1974. Minneapolis.

St. Constantine's Ukrainian Catholic Church. Dedication Souvenir Book. 1972. Minneapolis.

*St. Constantine's Ukrainian Catholic Church-Religious Art. [1995?] Minneapolis.*

*St. Mary's Orthodox Cathedral-100th Anniversary 1887–1987.* Minneapolis.

Scherer, Herbert. "Tickets to Fantasy." *Hennepin County History Magazine,* Fall 1987.

Schopf, Imogene Erie. "Reminiscences of Lowry School." *Minneapolis Argus,* 16 Aug 1978.

Shaffer, Glenda M. *Over The Years at Logan Park.* Minneapolis Park and Recreation Board. Minneapolis: Omega Press, 6 Aug 1992.

Shutter, Rev. Marion. *Gateway to the Northwest.* Chicago: S. J. Clarke Publishing Co., 1923.

Soine, Richard & Lee Hanson. *Northeast* sponsored by Project Challenge Northeast Area High School students, Northeast Neighborhood House, Chris Skjervold-MPS

Ethnic Cultural Center, Minnesota Folklife Society, Mr. A. Miskell-Jiffy Print 1978.

Stipanovich, Joseph. *City of Lakes: An Illustrated History of Minneapolis* Woodland Hills, CA: Windsor Publications, 1982.

Thornley, Stew. *Basketball's Original Dynasty: The History of the Lakers*. Minneapolis: Nodin Press, 1989.

Ueland, Brenda. "What Goes On Here." *Minneapolis Times,* 1944.

Wilcox Motor Car Co. *Minnesota History*, Fall 1972.

Wolniewicz, Richard. *Ethnic Persistence in Minneapolis*. Minnesota Project on Ethnic America. 1973.

Worcester, Michael R. "From the Land of the Golden Grain." *Hennepin History*, Fall 1992.

Zalusky, Joseph W. "The East Side Fire." *Hennepin County History,* Spring 1960.

# Photo Credits

Minnesota Historical Society, Cover, 12, 15, 18; Jacoby, 21, 22, 23L&R, 26, 27, 30, 33; Gordon Ray, 39, 46, 50, 54, 55, 59, 60; L Mills & Bell, 60R, 61, 68, 69, 73; C.P. Gibson, 74; F.L. Mortimer, 75, 77L&R, 78, 81, 83, 84; F.B. Brown, 86; Illustrative Photography, 87; Norton & Peel, 90, 93, 107, 119; *Minneapolis Journal*, 126, 128, 129 *Minneapolis Journal*, 138, 142, 145, 153L&R, 156, 157

Author's Collection, 10L&R, 14, 16, 17, 40, 80, 82

Courtesy of Minneapolis Board of Education, Facilities Department, 12, 67, 104, 135, 139L&R, 145, 150, 165, 167

Minneapolis Public Library, Minneapolis Collection, 24, 28, 38, 56, 63, 67, 72, 88, 118, 120, 126, 130, 150, 159

Hennepin County History Center, 24L&R and map in front of book.

Story of a Hundred Years-St. Anthony of Padua, 32, 33

Doug Kieley, Photographer, 34, 36, 42, 44, 48, 49

Centennial of St. Boniface, 35

Courtesy of Emanuel Evangelical, 37

The Northeaster, page 16 July 27, 1988, 43

St.Cyril's 90th Anniversary Booklet, 45

St. Mary's Orthodox 100th Anniversary, 47

St. Constantine's Dedication Book, 49

Holy Cross Centennial Parish Book, 51

Notre Dame De Minneapolis, Our Lady of Lourdes Book, 148

St. Paul Pioneer Press, John Doman, page 8B, Nov. 21, 1982, 57

Edison Yearbook 1930, 1935, 1944, 52, 64, 65, 66

Leibenberg & Kaplan Papers, Northwest Architectural Archives, University of Minnesota Libraries, 72, 79

Jerry Nelson, Photographer, 76 L&R, 80, 82, 85, 89, 92L&R, 113

Courtesy of Minneapolis Community Development Agency, 91, 108, 112L&R; *St.Anthony Falls Rediscovered*, Riverfront Development Coordination Board 1980

Courtesy of Guil Parsons, Edison Hall of Fame Scrapbook, 94, 99, 101, 102, 103L&R, 106 L&R

Eastside High Yearbook 1906, 106, 107

Over the Years at Logan Park, 116, 123

Courtesy of Olga Pawluk, 25, 144

Courtesy of Wilfred Leitschuh, 24, 107, 160, 163

Courtesy of Aaron Carlson, 71

Courtesy of Bud Blackey, 73

Courtesy of Harriet Krawczyk, 83

Courtesy of Surdyk's Liquor, 91

Courtesy of Don Carlson, 97

Courtesy of Zig Bishop, 101

Courtesy of Anna Biennias, 124

Courtesy of Connie Szczech, 128

Courtesy of Jean Kobus, 133

Courtesy of Sam Mancino, 137

Courtesy of Pat Eaton, 140

Courtesy of Bob Berny, 142

Courtesy of Evelyn Lund, 147

Courtesy of Don Risk, 149

Courtesy of Carol Brecht, 152

Courtesy of Scherer Brothers, 88

Courtesy of Charles Snelson, 155

Northeast Sun Press 1976, 141

Northeast, A History By Project Challenge, 164

*I'm Mama D, Shut Up and Listen*, 167, 168, 169

# Index

# About the Author

Genny Kieley is the author of numerous short stories and memoirs. Her story "A House No Longer Lived In" appeared in the Polish American Journal in Buffalo, New York.

A Northeast Minneapolis native, she has always had an interest in local and ethnic history and is currently working on a novel embracing her Polish heritage.

Genny lives with her husband in Champlin, Minnesota. She attends creative writing and critiquing classes at The Writing Center in Brooklyn Park, Minnesota.